"Ormsby recounts the mishaps, muddles and p
daily life hard for Romanians, and even harder for outsiders. But through it all comes a strange sort of affection for a place, and its people, as they struggle to regain their sanity after the years of madness under Ceauşescu. If you're going to Romania, it's better than a guide book."

Ivor Gaber, *Tribune (UK)*

"Never Mind the Balkans, Here's Romania" highlights the confluence of Romania's deeply-entrenched cultural traditions as they meet the new freedoms, temptations and commercialism that come with being the newest nation in the European Union."

David Shepard, *www.restromania.com.*
Tourism website, *New South Wales, Australia*

"Romanian clichés treated with intelligence and a unique, subtle irony. This merits pride of place on any bookshelf."

Mihai Gădălean, Foaia Transilvană

"Romania is graced with two kinds of foreigner. One sort is here on corporate junkets. The other sort sticks. We're dug in deep. We live in the streets, talk with the locals and deal first-hand with their ways and institutions. Judging by his book, Mike Ormsby is a sticker of some distinction. His reports from the front line are precise, detailed and a joy to read."

Frank O'Connor, *Vivid (expat magazine, Romania)*

"Mike Ormsby sees Romania very clearly. Sometimes we surprise him, sometimes he challenges us. Nevertheless, he clearly appreciates our charisma, confidence and warmth."

Mihaela Spineanu, *Elle (Romania)*

"Romania has found itself a British Caragiale. The book makes you die laughing."

Raluca Ion, *Cotidianul*

Mike Ormsby was born in England in 1959. He attended University College Cardiff and visited Romania as a BBC reporter in 1994.

He returned to train journalists at BBC School in Bucharest until 1997 and has been based in Romania ever since.

His screenplay 'Hey, Mr DJ!' was filmed and released in Kigali in 2007 and topped the bill at Rwanda's first Hillywood Film Festival. His short script 'Enfants Dits Sorciers' was filmed in Kinshasa in 2002. He is a columnist for Playboy.

Mike and his wife Angela Nicoară live and work around the world but hope to spend more time at their home in the hills of Transylvania, one day.

These stories are based on fact. Spooky but true.

Mike Ormsby

Never Mind the Balkans, Here's Romania

Nicoaro Books

ISBN-13: 978-1477465363
www.mikeormsby.net
lupa.capi@gmail.com
Twitter: @OrmsbyMike
Interior print design by Booknook.biz
Cover design by www.designforwriters.com

Acknowledgements

Thank you to my extended Romanian family and friends for helpful feedback.

Above all, I am indebted to my wife Angela Nicoară for her editing, suggestions and constant support. Also, to Maria and Ferdinant for wonderful summers *la ţară* and gossip from *Radio Şanţ*; to my three sisters-in-law: Nicoleta Nicoară in Zurich, Veronica Nicoară and Cristina Nicoară in New York; to Adrian, Cristina & Sarah Prohaska for hikes and yikes in Transylvania; to Horea & Imelda Sălăjan in Jakarta, and Dana & Jerome Leroy in Kigali.

Thank you to my family in England: Vera Ormsby, Eddie & Andrea Ormsby, Margaret & Derek Martindale, Colette & Brian Cooper, and my cousin Ray Ormsby.

I am grateful to Rupert Wolfe-Murray for opening a door, and to you too, if I forgot.

Mike Ormsby
Bucharest
7.7.2012

Contents

For my parents

Can you picture what will be, so limitless and free ?

Jim Morrison

Preface

In early December 2006, a few weeks before Romania's accession to the EU, an item about tourism was broadcast on the BBC World Service, in Romanian. The journalist asked an official what he planned to do about allegations of high prices, poor service and bad hygiene in some of Romania's hotels. By way of reply, the official told the reporter that the hotels were full and if he cared to try booking a room, he would discover it was not possible.

Jogging Is Good for You

I tie my running shoes in the elevator, on the way down to the lobby. I leave the apartment block and trot towards the big crossroads. The traffic is heavy and loud. Horns beep, lights flash, tyres squeal – business as usual for central Bucharest at 5pm. The weather has a bite to it: 3° C, with a sharp breeze blowing north-east from Bulgaria. I stop at the kerb, flexing on my heels to warm the calf muscles. I hitch up my socks and pull down my baseball cap to keep wind from my eyes. A big dusty Mercedes passes by. A guy in black leather leans out and yells at me:

"Gay!"

Heads turn nearby, at the bus stop. *Cheers mate.* The traffic lights change and I scoot across puddles, trying to look butch. Not easy in a lime green top and black Lycra tights.

Tonight I'll do 7 miles. That's about four laps of the Parliament – aka Ceauşescu's Palace of the People – second biggest building in the world or something. I nod at the guard on the first gate, hoping he might recognize me by now. But it's a different guard tonight. He stares back fish-eyed, as if we're in a spy movie.

A sleek black car suddenly appears behind him, zooming for the exit. The car is side on to me. I am on the driver's right, but he's staring left as he approaches, busy watching the oncoming traffic so he can pull out as soon as possible. He almost hits me. I skid to a halt and skip around the back of his car. I rap knuckles on his boot, twice, just enough to get his attention. His head jerks around. As I pass his door, I splay two fingers and jab them towards my eyes – *look properly next time*. He glowers at me and screeches off into the traffic.

At the next exit, less official than the previous one, there is no gate house and no security guard. A small dusty brown car kangaroos from the darkness. It's a Dacia, worse for wear. This driver is also looking left, waiting for a gap in the traffic. No chance. He slows down and stops. But as I run past the front of his car, it suddenly and inexplicably surges forward and rams into my left leg, knocking me off balance. I yelp in surprise. Luckily for me, the driver brakes and spins his head towards me. His eyes are wide, his mouth drops open. He gazes at me through the windscreen. He looks like a little fish in a bowl, puzzled by my world. I jab fingers at my eyes, yell at him to *look right, next time.* He's speechless. As I run off, he blasts his horn. Evidently, it was my fault.

I jog downhill, taking it easy for the next 500 meters. As I turn the corner into Constitution Square, a familiar, dry, crunching sound echoes across the vast semi-circle of cobbles and concrete. A sleek BMW has torpedoed into the back of a Jaguar. Steam hisses, a headlight rolls across the road like a glass eye. The drivers eject from their seats and start yelling at each other. Traffic grinds to a halt and then the horns start: an endless cacophony, like bleating sheep.

I keep going. A well-dressed woman stands with an expensive-looking dog, its face like a cabbage. She gazes into space as the dog plops a steaming stool onto a neatly-clipped verge. Then she walks away, dragging the dog. I watch to see if she will produce a plastic bag to scoop the poop. But she doesn't.

I turn the next corner, where cars, trucks, buses and big motorbikes are lined up at the lights, revving. Some of the drivers evidently like music – I can hear it from fifty yards. On the next stretch, empty cars sit smack in the middle of the pavement as far as I can see. But none of the cars has a parking ticket. To get by, I must run in the gutter. Buses and trucks roar past me in the gloom. At the next corner, I find a Renault buried in a wall, its bonnet concertina'd.

Running alongside the Senate, I'm somewhat surprised to find three cars driving straight at me, down the wide pavement. Presumably they don't want to queue in the traffic, on the street nearby, like everyone else. I yell at them and wave my arms, hoping they'll slow down.

They brake, perhaps thinking I'm a traffic cop in my lime green top. As I edge past, between the crawling cars and the Parliament wall, I notice the last one has DEP plates. That means the driver is a Deputy, a Romanian MP, probably heading home after a hard day's democracy.

There are still a few miles to go.

Europeans Are Stupid

I'm scared. My stomach is in a knot. I'm in the back of a car, in rural Romania. It's midnight. Pitch black outside, fields and trees and muddy ditches all around. Friends of friends are giving me a ride home. But she's driving fast, far too fast.

She sees the sharp bend too late and our car almost catapults into a field. They laugh, her and her husband, because they're young Romanians with jobs and money, style and brains. I ask her to slow down. They laugh again.

"Don't you have insurance?" asks the husband.

"I have experience," I reply.

"Is that British humour?"

"I'm not joking. Your wife is going to cause an accident, she'll crash the car."

She turns and gawks at me like I've lost my tiny mind.

"How can I," she says, "when there are no other cars around?"

I don't answer. If that's logic, I'm Donald Duck.

"We drove across Europe this summer," adds her husband with a bored yawn, flexing his arms behind his head. The wife glances back at me, smiling.

"In Monte Carlo," she says, "we paid forty euros for two espressos!"

Then she skids into another bend.

"Please, slow down?" I ask. I sound like a beggar.

"You know what?" continues the husband, "you Europeans are stupid."

I try to laugh.

"Really, why is that?" I ask. I'm curious to hear how travel has broadened his mind. He shakes his head and replies:

"Because you stick to the speed limit even when there are no cops around!"

They giggle and grin at each other, cocky as hell. I stare into the dark night. Is there any point in telling them that in Europe, the idea is that we should police ourselves? Probably not.

Twenty minutes later, on a fast and tricky four-lane highway, our driver is doing 140 kph when she suddenly slams on the brakes. The tyres scream in protest. We lurch forward in our seats. Papers fly off the back shelf. The car screeches to a halt. She points at a rabbit sitting in the road, staring at our headlights. Like Bugs Bunny. The husband is speechless.

"Look, there's a rabbit. I don't want to kill it," explains the wife.

Huge trucks thunder past from behind, horns BLARING and lights FLASHING. I'm terrified. Any second now, we're dead.

The husband yells at her in Romanian and English, as if for my benefit.

"You stupid f*****g bitch! F*** the rabbit!! Start the f*****g car, before we all get f*****g killed!!!"

She does, and we don't.

Anaesthesia

The dentist sticks the needle into the back of my mouth. The pain makes me jump, as if he just put electrodes on my head and flipped a switch. My hips rise off the chair, involuntarily. I yelp like a beaten dog.

"Going somewhere?" he asks.

I shake my head, sweating. He smiles sweetly.

"Did I hit the nerve?" he asks. I nod my head, weakly. He smiles again.

"Do you know," he murmurs, "there are more nerve endings connected to your bite than to almost any other part of your body?"

I shake my head, blinking in the bright light. My chest is pounding.

"Try to relax," he tells me.

I exhale slowly, watching and waiting. He stares through double-glazed windows at Bucharest's ancient balconies and modern blocks. He looks puzzled, as if trying to retrace the conversation. Ah, he remembers.

"Something else about Jews," he continues, "not that I don't like them, but they're very clannish. Not to mention rich. I'm sure they want to control the world."

I tell him *no,* that's the Americans, closely followed by the Chinese. We Brits gave up a long time ago.

He chuckles and shoves cotton wadding into my mouth. The anaesthesia is taking effect and after twenty minutes I'm slobbering saliva through liverish lips. He's still muttering at me about Jews-this and Jews-that, as he drills at my teeth. It's a big job, my third visit this week. Two days ago he pinned me down for seven hours. But like any good dentist, he's alert to the client's reactions. He sees me roll my eyes and stands back, observing me over the top of his white paper mask, two dark eyes glittering like onyx.

"Do I sound disrespectful?" he asks.

"You sound like a Nazi," I mumble.

He chuckles again. This time, it bugs me. So I tell him I don't care for anti-Semitic garbage. But he just laughs and tells he likes tormenting his patients when they're under anaesthesia, because they can't reply. He winks at me. That does it.

"The anaesthesia is in your head", I mutter, as best I can. "Your brain is doped with racist ideology. The question is why."

He sits down on his stool and admits it's a good point. But he has a theory to explain it.

"I hated the Communists so much, for years I would only read right-wing books. Politics, history, novels – I wanted to kill Ceauşescu. I'd even kill Iliescu if I met him today, swear to God! I picture him in my chair, suffering."

He sighs and explains that after the Revolution in 1989, he stopped reading. Instead, he focused on dentistry, got good clients and a big car.

"I know it's wrong but I'm still blocked, mentally. Maybe you can help?"

He seems genuinely concerned.

"Only if you listen," I reply.

His slim, pretty assistant walks in.

"See this girl?" the dentist says, in a loud voice. "She wants to f**k me."

The assistant arranges the shiny tools on his tray and gives him a weary smile. He smiles back and tells her: "Your tits are too small."

When We Get Organized

I need tea, strong black tea. Not this Lipton's Yellow Label stuff that dominates Romania's supermarkets and tastes like sawdust. I want real tea – Twinings or Tetley or Fair Trade or something. So I phone home. My mother – a serious tea-drinker – clucks in sympathy down the line and agrees to post some from England. But she sounds concerned.

"Will it reach you OK? Won't there be problems at the Post Office, in Romania?"

"No," I reply, "Now that we're in the EU, all EU mail is delivered to our doors. Or so I've heard."

It certainly sounds like a good idea. No more little grey tickets in the mailbox, no more endless queues at the Post Office. Three weeks later, tongue hanging out, I call again. *Mother, where's my teabags?*

"I sent them the day you asked," she replies.

Later in the week I open my mailbox and find a little grey ticket. It says I've got a package from England. It's at the Post Office, so come and get it.

I grab my coat. It's either an hour's walk or twenty euros in a cab. I decide to walk, enjoy the sunny day. En route, two tough-looking guys try to hustle me who-knows-what. I feel like saying *Excuse me, is this 1990 or 2007?* But I've had enough smacks in Romania already.

At the Post Office, clerks are busy stamping forms – it sounds like Tchaikovsky's *1812*.

I hand in my little grey ticket and join the long grey queue. A stubbly man in shades yaps loudly on his mobile. A glamorous lady with four-inch heels pulls at her tight denim jeans. Through a doorway, a woman the size of a house stands knee-deep in a room of brown paper parcels, scratching her head and sucking something that makes her mouth go round and round like a washing machine.

After twenty minutes, somebody in the queue gets called on the intercom. After thirty minutes, somebody else gets called. After fifty minutes, I'm still leaning at the marble counter, wondering when it will be my turn. Then I notice that some folks who arrived later than me are now leaving with parcels and smiley faces. How come? I go and check. The big lady says *yes,* we *found your parcel, but you have to wait.* After one hour and fifteen minutes they announce my name on the intercom, slowly and deliberately, as if to say *who-made-this-up?*

I go and get my parcel. I'm surprised to discover it is quite a small one – small enough to fit in my mailbox – so why didn't they deliver it? The big lady makes me open the parcel so she can see what's inside. A big man in a security uniform comes to see. They seem a bit surprised to find only tea bags. I sign a form and tell them I'm surprised they didn't deliver it.

"Doesn't mail from the EU come to our boxes now?" I ask.

"Yes," replies the big lady, "when we get organized."

"So when will that be?" I ask, as nicely as I can, "Next month, six months maybe?"

She stamps my form with a loud thud and says: "Yes, when we get organized."

Lupa Capitolina

I like that statue. Romulus and Remus suckling beneath a she-wolf. It sits in the middle of a boulevard off Piaţa Romana. The original was made in 6 BC, an Etruscan bronze, whatever that means, now in the Conservatory Palazzo in Rome. In 1918, Italian diplomats gave five bronze copies to their Latin cousins in Romania to mark the Great Union, the birth of Romania as a state. One copy was unveiled in Bucharest and I'm looking at it, all black and shiny in the rain.

I'm in a phone box, calling an animal shelter about a sick dog. The one I see every day, not far from the statue. It hops around for scraps, brown fur falling out in clumps. As I dial, it is watching me from a patch of rough grass, as if it knows what I'm up to.

The dog is just one of thousands, the offspring of those abandoned by bemused Romanians when President Ceauşescu forced whole communities into blocks of flats, part of his plan to destroy and rebuild the capital. Or so they say. The dogs have been breeding ever since. Not to mention barking and biting. Once, they even killed a man. Down the phone, I explain that this particular dog is starving, has a severe case of mange and a bad leg.

"And what am I supposed to do?" asks the guy on the other end of the line. I'm puzzled by his tone.

"Is this Wet Nose, the NGO that helps street dogs?" I ask.

He growls back in broken English:

"Yes, but that one needs care and attention!"

I'm starting to feel like Alice down the rabbit hole.

"That's why I rang," I say.

He tells me to ring back in ten minutes. When I do, he barks a number and hangs up before I can clarify who it's for, maybe the Veterinary College? I have an idea that Wet Nose has links with students. I saw something about it on the glittering website with the cute logo. I call the new number, wondering.

A lady answers. It's some kind of animal charity hospice. She is refreshingly polite and makes helpful suggestions to treat the mangy dog. But she keeps saying *if you can afford it, that is.*

"So it's not free?" I ask, puzzled. "You're not funded by a grant or something?"

"No," she sighs, "we're private. You pay 15 euros per day for board and 30 euros per treatment. But a skin condition can take months. Plus, you have to bring the dog to us and catching them can be a bit tricky."

Outside, the skinny brown dog stares at me as if to say *you bet.*

"Sounds expensive," I reply.

I probably sound like a complete dope. Maybe I am.

"Have you tried Wet Nose?" asks the friendly lady from the hospice. I try not to laugh. "They sent me to you," I reply, looking down at my shoes. Defeat hangs over my head.

"Yes, they do that a lot," she says, sounding a bit weary of it all.

"What else do they do?" I ask, thinking about that nice website. But she maintains a diplomatic silence. When I look up, my mangy brown dog has found a friend under the statue.

Chivas Life

Something's not right. Cătălin is putting far too much food into our supermarket trolley. Weekend supplies for three people? No way. What's he up to? As he reaches for a second bottle of Chivas Regal, I slide alongside to find out.

"Hey Cătă," I ask, "so much food for you, Ruxi and me?"

He avoids my eye and offers an impish grin:

"Actually, there'll be ten of us. Didn't I mention it?"

He looks rather pleased with himself. I try my best to smile. He moves to the dairy section. I follow him, wondering why he promised *a quiet weekend, walks and talks; we gotta catch up after eight years apart!* Wasn't that the idea? But now he's moved the goalposts, and invited a football team. He looks into our shopping trolley. He seems puzzled. He lifts out a pack of Romanian butter and holds it up.

"Did you put this in?" he asks.

I nod. Cătălin pulls a face: *oh dear.* Then he replaces the butter with a Danish brand, three times the price. He wraps an arm around my shoulder, like father and son, and guides the trolley into the next aisle. He leans closer, speaking quietly.

"Let me do the shopping, OK?"

I shrug and try to look grateful. Something's changed.

"You're our guest!" coos Ruxi, his good-looking young girlfriend. "Cătă's told me all about you," she adds, vaguely.

I tag along like a kid who just got adopted. Ruxi has bright green eyes, blonde hair and an infectious giggle. She hoists her slim body onto the handle of the trolley, high heels dangling. She pouts at the rag dolls as we pass the toy section.

"So cute," she purrs.

At the checkout, our bill is over $ 250. Middle-aged Romanians with tired eyes stare at my rich young buddy, who slips a VISA card to the assistant and mutters *whack it on the business*.

A little later, we leave the city behind us, heading for the countryside. Cătă drives his yellow Porsche like a fighter pilot. I ask him to slow down.

"Why, don't you like going fast?" he asks.

I'm tempted to say *try running 10 km in 47 minutes.* But I don't. His muscular Doberman leans forward from the back seat and licks my ear, for being a good boy. I turn around and spot Ruxi's Beetle, just a dot in the distance. She's taking her time with a car full of girls. They'll meet us there. Our Porsche roars through a village. Cătă blasts his horn at a skinny old guy on a wobbly bicycle and says "The stupid motherfucker."

We reach the cottage at 1 pm. In the yard, Cătă cranks up the music, does a little dance and slaps beef and salmon on the barbecue. By 3 pm, he's drunk half a bottle of Chivas and his eyes resemble boiled tomatoes. Buddies arrive in slick cars. They wear ragged jeans and T-shirts with punky fonts. Their hair is gelled like they slept in the park. They roll cardboard tubes of single malt whisky across the table, Glen-this and Glen-that. They tell their girlfriends to fetch glasses. They cluster around Cătă at the coals, basking in his glow. Ruxi stays indoors, says it's too cold.

Cătă spends two hours playing chess with his back to me. At 9 pm, a guest asks me who I am and what I do. I briefly update him on ten years in Europe, Africa, Asia and America. He changes the subject. Ruxi reappears and ambles around the garden on the phone to Mum, who is writing her college essay. When Cătă returns from a midnight motorbike ride, barely able to stand, he feeds salmon steak to his wide-eyed Doberman and then squats beside me, pouring more Chivas.

"So dude," he asks, "what was it you wanted to talk about?"

Lucky

I'm in love with Transylvania. I love the way the horizon rolls, I love how the Carpathian Alps soar like a tidal wave two thousand metres high. I love the sound of the words: *Făgăraş (fugger-ash) Ucea (oo-chay-ah), Braşov (brash-ov).* I love the timeless images of rural life flashing past the window of my train. A shepherd leans on his stick, wearing a fleecy coat the size of a small car. A ramshackle wooden wagon jolts down a muddy track, lead by a prancing, skinny black horse with blinkers and a faded rosette. Mucky kids squat in ditches, tossing pebbles into pools. Stout women in headscarves carry wood or chat over a fence, tough as old boots. Wizened old men sip from small glasses, playing chess in their rumpled black suits, white shirts and black hats.

I arrive in Sibiu and friends meet me at the station. I twist and turn on the back seat of their shiny new Dacia Logan, checking on the small, ancient city. Several years since I was here. It feels the same as last time, yet looks different. Tiled roofs still pitch at odd angles, their ventilation slats watching the town like sleepy eyes. Citizens still stroll with an unhurried gait, born of resilience. But construction cranes loom over us and cement-mixer trucks trundle behind glittering new offices. There are day-glo posters, designer shops. Something seems to be tugging at the place, the wind of change maybe.

Adina and Gabriel drop me at my hotel and we agree to meet later for dinner at their home. I ride the elevator up to my floor. From my room I take in the majestic view of wobbly chimney stacks and far hills. The sun is still up, but not for much longer. I need exercise after my five-hour train ride. So I unpack my running gear, get changed and head out from the hotel, taking back-streets I haven't seen in years. I jog past a tiny hunting museum and then off towards a vast park with mountains in the distance. I know where I'm going and how long it takes. I know this place, maybe it knows me.

My route takes me past a clutch of run down houses with rubbish strewn outside. I wave gloved fingers at two dark-eyed little lads standing around a large sloping pit. They wave back and crouch down over a small puppy, tickling it with a length of wire. The tiny dog rolls belly up.

After half an hour of snow and slush, my feet are soaked and freezing. I turn back. Soon I see the kids again. They are throwing a bundle of rags in the air and kicking it as it falls. But it falls too fast. Then I hear a pitiful wailing, an animal in distress. As I get closer, I discover that the bundle of rags is actually the puppy, with the wire now looped around its neck, in a noose. The bigger lad grabs the end of the wire, tosses the dog in the air. The younger lad kicks it as it falls. The dog yelps. The kids giggle and start again. I stop, peering through the rain, making sure they are doing what I think they are doing. I run towards them, snatch the pup and shove it into my top. They gawk at me. I curse them. They curse me back. I run off with *'F*** America'* ringing in my ears. I turn and shout *I'm not American,* as if it matters.

Over dinner, my friends agree to keep the puppy.

"We'll call it Lucky!" says hazel-eyed Adina. She has a caring, intelligent manner and I'm grateful for her kindness. She urges her handsome husband to build a kennel in the communal yard of their block. Gabi grins and pours more *palinca*, his supremely potent home-made eau-de-vie, up to 70 percent proof. Three days later, they drop me at the station. Adina holds little Lucky at my window, waving a stubby black paw. He wriggles and chews her fingers.

After six months Gabi calls me, sobbing down the line. He says the dog grew big and fast, dug the ground, barked a lot and took four days to die when a neighbour poisoned its food.

Not So Lucky

I remember this place, always will. I should have kept my mouth shut. Play with fire, right? But that was then. Now it's 2007, and I walk through Gara de Nord feeling older and wiser.

The big railway station looks so different today – modern, revamped. Shiny kiosks bulge with glossy mags, rows of chocolate and stacks of snacks. Men in suits chat on mobile phones. Glamorous girls laugh and joke, swigging Fanta. Ticket collectors amble in smart uniforms, hats perched at a rakish angle. Not like the old days, when poverty assailed the senses at every step: the stink of vagrants, ragged kids sucking plastic bags, feral dogs snapping at dust storms down the track.

Today I stand and wait as a shiny train pulls in. Middle-aged passengers climb down lugging heavy bags; lithe young guys skip past with neat Armani knapsacks, fake or otherwise.

"Hey Mike!"

The voice sounds familiar. I spot David through the crowd, rolling towards me like a sailor home from sea. We shake hands and hug. He's still got those Welsh rugby arms.

"Look at you!" he jokes, as we thread through happy families and tearful lovers. I wonder if David will mention *that day*. And yes he does, as soon as we reach the main concourse. He stops under the big station clock, exactly where it happened.

"Hey Mike!" he says, a grin splitting his tanned, beery face. "Do you remember?"

I nod and look up at the clock.

In 1994, the big American wore sandals. He was holding a wad of dollars. The Romanian guys were pestering him to change money. So I walked past and said: "Don't" from the corner of my mouth. The American tailed me like a puppy, as I explained the risks. "Thanks buddy!" he said.

He wandered off. I was waiting for David, the Welsh charity worker from Craiova. I was holding a huge black vase. Some dark Romanian guy asked how much it cost. I realized he wasn't checking the vase, he was checking me. He turned away, as if signalling – but to whom?

Then David had arrived with his mates – big rugby types and two women. We walked towards the clock, heading out. Until a stocky, middle-aged Romanian stopped me; leather coat, unshaven, slicked hair. Tough-looking with dark protruding eyes. He smiled and asked quietly:

"Do you know me, friend?"

I shook my head and he spoke again.

"Did I ever hurt you?"

"No," I replied, not liking the tone of his question. It seemed to have implications.

"So why did you tell the American not to change money?" he asked.

My Welsh pals looked at me, puzzled. I felt like a lamb facing a lion. My heart was thumping as I answered.

"Because I know what you do."

It was the best I could offer. The Romanian guy gave me a quick grin, calm and friendly.

"Do you? Well now, my friend, let me tell you something. You must never…"

Then my world exploded. I was flying backwards in slow motion. Moments later I hit the ground and saw the big vase shatter into a thousand pieces nearby. My jaw seemed to have been ripped from my skull, like a horse had kicked it off. I heard screams and yells. I couldn't move, only watch and listen. I felt strong hands – someone pulling me up. I felt blood pouring from my mouth and watched it trickle down my jacket. I saw my beefy attacker walking away, flexing his shoulders, tugging his leather cuffs. Then I heard David gasp in admiration.

"What a punch!"

"I think he bust my jaw," I mumbled.

My pals dusted me down and stuffed tissues into my mouth. Then they marched me out of the station and into the nearest cab, keen to get away as fast as possible. I sat on the back seat and as we drove off, I saw the big American in sandals talking to the guy who had whacked me, showing his dollars. I put my head in my hands, to stop it falling off. No good. I leaned back to watch white clouds roll across a blue sky.

"He pulled a knife," murmured David, "He was going to stab you, on the ground."

"What?" I whispered, with blood pooling under my tongue.

"And when we stopped him, he said: 'Tell your friend – next time, not so lucky'."

But that was then. Now it's 2007 and the big guys just smile and offer taxis, at twice the price.

The President Wants to Meet You

"Why?" I ask.

My neighbour Lumi beckons me towards the elevator on the tenth floor of our apartment block. A chilly wind howls up the old concrete shaft, bringing smells of damp and fried onions. Below us sit dozens of apartments, scores of residents. So how come he wants me?

"It's about your request," she replies.

I lock my flat and follow her down the dimly-lit corridor, past a small jungle of thrusting vegetation, courtesy of Mrs. Popa, the friendly, anxious widow who lives next door.

The President's office is on the ground floor. It's about the size of a shoe-box but already filling with residents when we arrive: mostly male, middle-aged and well-dressed in 1970s East European Communist chic: white shirts buttoned to the neck, dark blue caps like naval captains, baggy grey suits with one lapel in Hungary and the other in Ukraine. A couple of ladies huddle against a radiator wearing fluffy jumpers, thick socks and flip flops. They look but don't smile.

At the end of the room end sit three men in a row, like a panel of experts. Mr. Vlaicu, the Administrator, is on the right, his prominent forehead and silky grey hair shining under the neon strip. He fixes me with baby blue eyes, as if to say *who invited you.* On the left side sits the Vice-President, an earnest-looking young man with three chins, two notepads and one pencil.

In the middle sits Mr. Ilie, the President of the Block. Mr. Ilie is handsome, aged sixty-plus, with wide shoulders, brooding eyes and a military stiffness. He stares at Lumi over gold-rimmed spectacles and mutters to the VP, who scribbles in his pad. Vlaicu coughs, silence descends. The residents sit up straight. It's starting.

After twenty minutes of babble about The-Brown-Water-Situation, Why-The-Elevator-Jams, Who-Will-Tell-The-Chinese-To-Move-Their-Van, and Did-That-German-Sell-His-Apartment-Yet, Mr. President flashes an official smile in my direction. His teeth protrude and have an odd colour, as if he smokes too much. Either that or they are made of wood.

"The English have a request?" he asks, encouragingly.

Heads turn in my direction and eleven sets of rheumy eyes look me up and down, as if expecting treachery. Lumi intervenes, explaining that *The English* would like to apply for a parking space. The panel exchange glances. Vlaicu the Administrator purses his lips and shakes his head. *No way.* The President smiles diplomatically and asks Lumi: "Anything else?"

I tell him I want to discuss my electricity bill, which is way too high.

"Because you installed new radiators!" snaps Administrator Vlaicu. "I've seen them!"

I remember his friendly visits a few months ago, when he complimented me on how warm they were, asked me how many I had. I thought he wanted some himself. It seems I was wrong.

"But Mr. Vlaicu," I reply, "They're energy-efficient, remember? I've got documents…"

I offer a sheet of data from my pocket. The President takes it, eyes aflame.

"Documents?!" he scowls. "We won't sink to your game!"

Then he's off, yelling and waving and rolling his eyes. The VP is scribbling so fast, his pencil breaks. Vlaicu quickly slips him a chewed biro, lest history be unwritten. We argue for ten minutes. But they won't reduce my bill, because my radiators are hotter than theirs. Even though mine are cheaper, and I can prove it.

Later in the elevator, Lumi counsels me, burning with indignation.

"What they're up to is illegal!"

"What will they do with my cash?" I ask.

"Reduce their own bills, give themselves a Christmas bonus?" she replies, folding her arms. The elevator jams between the third and fourth floors. We wait for a bit, but it's stuck fast.

"If it drops, we die," Lumi sighs. "I'm serious. It happens."

I gaze at our reflections in the polished steel door, thinking about the nice pasta I was planning for tonight. Lumi pulls out her mobile phone.

"I'd better call Vlaicu," she says, prodding her keypad. "He likes rescuing people."

offoce@operanb.ro

Finally, I find somewhere to go in the evening. Somewhere free of cigarette-puffing, shade-wearing babes and spikey-haired guys with steel studs in their eyeballs? Somewhere middle-aged couples won't offer loud reviews from two rows back? It's the opera, and a long time since I saw one. I'm not a huge fan but Bucharest has a good name and the opera house looks magnificent all lit up at night. That's what gives me the idea, seeing all those people emerging, yapping like they've had a good time, or lost the plot.

So, one sunny day I wander down to buy a ticket. Even the approach road is elegantly laid out, with a long garden up the middle, benches and flower beds. I pull at the long brass handle of huge glass doors and enter to find a ticket booth tucked inside the lobby. In the booth sits a lady in a woolly jumper fielding telephone calls whilst reading a novel. I wait outside, cupping my palms against a second set of glass doors, cool to the touch. Beyond them, lies a majestic lobby of red carpets, curtains, chandeliers and wide marble staircases. It looks magical. I can't wait.

The ticket-lady closes her novel and explains my options. I decline Mozart's fussy tunes and convoluted comedies in favour of Verdi's beefy *Aida.* There's a slim screen on the wall above the ticket-booth, modern or what? The ticket-lady pokes at her keyboard and I watch the screen above my head. A tiny white square turns blue: that's my seat, near the front. How efficient.

I hurry home to surf the opera's impressive website, lots of red and gold. Eager to find out more, I subscribe to the email *Newsletter* and click on the tab saying *Get Involved.* Then I click on *Virtual Tour – Panoramic Video.* I'm hoping to see the main hall, the stage, even my seat. But the panoramic video doesn't work. Disappointed, I click the *Contact Us* tab and fill in a little box, to ask why. The site flashes a friendly message: *We'll reply as soon as possible!*

Three days later, I get an email: *offoce@operanb.ro is not a valid address.* On a hunch, I write again, tweaking their address to '*office*'. My hunch pays off and moments later I get an email containing the same message I saw on the website: *We'll reply as soon as possible!* Two weeks later, still nothing. So I write again, and this time I up the ante by adding:

> *I wish to buy 50 top-price tickets for VIPs from Vienna.*
> *But first I'd like to see the Hall on the Virtual Tour.*

Days pass. No reply. Not a peep. And still no *Newsletter*. And no details of how to *Get Involved.*

On the night, *Aida* is a treat. The hall glitters, the two leading ladies sing superbly, with eyes that burn and boobs that wobble. Great musicians, a dynamic conductor and stunning sets.

But what really catches my eye is the passion of a skinny female extra whose efforts seem to annoy a trio of her companions. Onstage, in full view of the audience, these three large ladies spend twenty minutes muttering and smirking between themselves, edging her out of the lime-light. At the final curtain, the exuberant extra now looks bitterly upset, drained and close to tears. I have a feeling there's been a row backstage, a scene that Verdi did not write. I feel sorry for her. I feel like saying *don't worry, life was cruel to Aida too*. Maybe I'll email the official website, thank her for a top-class performance? Maybe she'll see it? No, most probably not.

Good Cop, Bad Cop

Clever guy, that Henri Coandă. His old planes look cool hanging from the ceiling of Henri Coandă Airport on the outskirts of Bucharest. So why do those Wright Brothers get all the credit – just because they're American? It seems unfair. I check my watch again, walking up and down the arrivals concourse. Where's Laura? Her flight landed ages ago, from Paris. Why the delay?

Five minutes later, she emerges through the sliding doors, with a face like a slapped ass. Even from twenty meters, I can tell she's pissed off – because of me? Maybe. You never know with Laura. She's young and brainy, tall and skinny, beautiful and hip. That's the good news, now the weather forecast: Laura is liable to explode, at any time, over nothing. So you'd best be nice. At least, that's how I remember it. Then again, I haven't seen my young Romanian friend since she was 16 and living in Brăila. Now she's 21, married and based in Noo Yawk Siddy. OK?

She's walking across the concourse. She's looking up at the ceiling. I stride towards her with my smile glued on and my arms open wide, hoping for a friendly hug. Instead, Laura shakes my hand and raises a well-plucked eyebrow.

"So did you, like, uh, bring a car? Or do we gotta take a fricken cab?"

In the back of the fricken cab, Laura brushes dust from her immaculate suede pumps – pink and brown, Diesel logo – and explains why she is *pissed.* Something to do with the airport.

"After the passport stuff, these Romanian cops stop me, with their *Poliţia de Frontieră* badges, right?"

I nod in sympathy, relieved that Laura's youthful anger is not directed at me. She squints through the taxi window, craning her neck at the endless construction projects on the busy road towards the city centre.

"There were two of them, a woman and a man," she mutters, shaking her head at some unspeakable crime. Then she stares at her pumps in silence.

"And?" I ask.

But Laura just frowns, taking her time – anger management maybe – before she replies.

"First, the woman cop says *where did you come from?* I tell her *Paris, from my sister's.* But she says, *no, I mean where did you start?* So I say *Noo Yawk.* Then the guy asks me if I live there and I say *sure I do.* And then he says *so you must be rich, if you live in New York and you have a sister in Paris?* I say *I'm not rich.* Then he smiles and says *really, what's in your bags?"*

Laura's heel is tapping hard against the taxi seat. She sips some Evian water, pushes her specs up her nose. "That's when they asked for the money," she snorts.

"What?" I ask. "Why?"

She gives me a pitiful look, like I need to wise up.

"Why d'ya think? Because they opened my bags! They saw my laptop and said *you got to give us something*. I said

I have no money. They said *New York, Paris? Think we're stupid?"*

"So did you pay them?" I inquire. Laura teases the silk headband off her scalp and shakes her hair free. It smells of apricots.

"You know what," she growls, "I come home after three years, to the same *fricken Romanian bullshit*, it makes me sick! Nothing's changed!"

"Did you pay?" I ask again. Laura laughs.

"No way! The woman cop said *you're cute and tired, we'll let you go. Just give my friend a coffee.* So I offered the guy $10, but he walked off. I guess it wasn't enough, asshole!"

Then Laura remembers something, and turns to look through the rear window.

"Hey, they changed the name of the airport!"

"Henri Coandă," I reply. She raises a thumb in appreciation.

"That's so cool," she says, smiling for the first time. "He was a clever dude. You know what he did, right?"

"Sure do, buddy," I reply, trying to affect a New York accent. Laura gives me a funny look and tells me it's a *real neat concourse, all them old planes.* But I tell her it's not fair. Romanians deserve more credit, more respect.

And Christmas Presents

I need help: an office assistant, someone reliable. Someone who knows how to get things done, speaks English, has relevant qualifications, experience and potential. So I draft a job ad, post it on some Bucharest websites and in the local press. Then I wait, checking my email, expecting a tsunami of applicants. Because the pay is decent and the work will not be too hard.

A week later, I've got fifteen CVs. I print them out, grab a coffee and sit in a comfy chair with a yellow highlighter pen (for the good bits) and red one (for the dodgy bits).

Flicking through the pile, I'm struck by two things. First, almost all the applicants are female. Second, almost every one has added a provocative photograph. Some tilt their heads sideways, as if to say *come and get me.* Some pout their ruby lips, as if for a kiss. One applicant has sent a full-length shot of herself in a little black dress with sequins and see-through shoulder straps, her hair tumbling onto tanned shoulders, as if she's applying for a job in a new casino. Another applicant confesses that *she would have to overcome her pride to take this job*. Having skimmed her work history, I have to wonder why. Another reveals that she knows she is *ideal for the job* because she *wants to travel the world.* Presumably, travelling to-and-from the photocopier will come as a disappointment. Elsewhere, I spot several 'graduates' of 2-week courses and a rash of dubious-sounding 'diplomas' from 3-day seminars on something-ism.

Only two males have applied. The first wants *a company car and a mobile phone*. He's *gonna work real hard* and *would of had like better grades but the thing is I dint finish coz I got kinda sick.* His English reads like an SMS sent from a skateboard. The other male applicant writes that he would like a company car, a mobile phone AND CHRISTMAS PRESENTS (in upper case font, just so I know). Bemused, I flick to his next page, half-expecting to find a long list entitled *Dear Santa Claus*. Christmas presents? Maybe he knows that some western companies in Romania shower their local employees with gifts and he's expecting the same from me? Then I remember something else. Although Christmas was officially banned during Communism, the Romanian state would provide its lucky workers with seasonal goodies, from *MoşGerilă* – Jack Frost – a white-bearded man in a baggy red suit. Apparently, the workers would take such gifts home to their kids – oranges, sweets, even clothes. Maybe that's it? But that was then.

Right now, it's twenty minutes since I started on the pile and I've listed four possible names. Trouble is, something's not right. Nobody cuts the mustard. It's like I'm going through the motions. So I take a break and stand at the window with my hands on top of my head, knuckles locked, gazing out at the Bucharest skyline where cranes swing and dust rises.

Surely there must be someone? How come these youngsters seem to have no idea how to apply for a job? I want to open the window and yell across the city rooftops: *Wake up, boys and girls!*

Then I get a brilliant idea. Maybe I should start a new training NGO, offering courses to final year students at every college in Romania: *How not to apply for a Job.* But, on the other hand, it's not my problem. I just need an office assistant, and time is ticking. I check my watch and walk back to my seat, eager to flip through the last five applicants. You never know.

The final CV hits me like a thunderbolt from heaven. Even the layout suggests superior intelligence. I wonder what planet she's from. I test her qualifications against my Wish List: *check, check.* I compare her CV with the rest, which are now slashed with my red ink. She's good. But something is missing. Then it dawns on me. Actually, nothing is missing. She just didn't send a photo, because I didn't ask. And frankly, right now, I don't care if she looks like ET.

I quickly read her CV again, just to make sure I'm not hallucinating. Then I pick up my phone and dial. Her name is Toni. I hope she's telling the truth.

Capra vecinului

Ioana seems happy, tapping a finger to gentle jazz music in the car. She turns to face me from the passenger seat, as the glittering lights of Zurich airport fade behind us.

"You'll like Switzerland," she says, her dark eyes flashing. She has glossy hair, clear skin and a trim physique. She wears a retro Adidas tracksuit – pale blue with brown stripes. She looks very different now to the hollow-cheeked student I knew years ago, back in Romania.

"It's different here," she adds.

Her husband Fritz guides the purring Audi towards a highway where a huge grey Mercedes slows down, making space for us to merge.

"In some ways," he murmurs, a discreet smile curling along his square jaw. He checks his rear-view mirror and flips his tail lights to thank the driver behind us. Fritz wears tiny spectacles with clear flexible arms that hook neatly behind his ears. He's quiet and business-like, hardly speaking as we speed towards the suburbs.

Ioana promises all sorts of adventures for my long weekend. But first, she has a job interview tomorrow morning – a chance to get some decent full-time work in her chosen field.

"Fitness trainer," she says, proudly, "At a nice health centre! My studies are paying off!"

She updates me on her qualifications in nutrition, aerobics, strength training, aqua-fit, Nordic skiing and plenty more. She's been busy since we last met, by the sound if it.

"How's your German?" I ask. But Fritz answers for her.

"It's pretty good, actually. She even learned *dialect*, and that's a tough call."

Next morning I sleep late, tired from my trip. By the time I rise, they're both gone. I mooch around the slick apartment, checking it out. The kitchen floor is warm – tiles heated from underneath? The tap water tastes fine. From the balcony I spot different bins for recycling. The neighbourhood looks neat and tidy. The air smells clean. It must be nice living here.

Fritz turns up at lunchtime, looking as if he's had enough of Swiss banking. He loosens his tie and prowls around the kitchen, hands on hips. Ioana follows him in, clearly upset. She dumps her sports bag and flops into the leather sofa, biting her lip. She looks ready to cry. Something's wrong. Maybe they've had a domestic.

"I'll call them," says Fritz. "What's their number?"

But Ioana shakes her head, giving him a feeble smile. "Forget it." Fritz catches my eye and explains. "She didn't get it, that job at the spa. They turned her down, for no good reason."

"The boss was nice at first," says Ioana. "She was German, seemed to like my CV. I thought I had the job. But then her assistant turned up – a Romanian woman. I thought she might be friendly but she wasn't, she was bossy. She said *your most important job will be cleaning the toilets, showers and changing rooms*. Then she said *you must sit at reception but never touch the cashbox. And be quick with the drinks tokens, or the Swiss will complain.*'"

Ioana rolls her eyes and tries to laugh, but it sounds bitter-sweet.

"Complain?" she repeats, "Swiss people hardly ever complain!"

Fritz frowns, making a frothy drink. He hands us a glass each. It tastes very good – thick and creamy banana with a cinnamon kick. Ioana takes a sip and gives him a tearful wink.

"Then what?" he asks, settling onto a high chrome stool at the breakfast bar.

"So then, that Romanian woman tried to impress me with her dialect skills," Ioana continues. "But she could hardly speak it! Just parrot phrases, even her German is pretty bad!"

"Did you tell her you don't want to be a receptionist?" I ask.

"Of course!" replies Ioana. "I told her I'm a fully-qualified wellness trainer. She told me *be quiet, pay attention.* But I couldn't after that. She left me in reception, told me *wait there.* Her boss came later and said *sorry but you're over-qualified and my Romanian colleague is worried about your lack of dialect*. I couldn't believe it. That's so unfair! I speak good dialect!"

Fritz drains his glass, lifts up a slim red telephone and turns to his unhappy wife.

"So, you're too-good-but-not-good-enough? How interesting. What's their number?"

Ioana rattles it off and he dials. We listen while he chats down the line in German. Then he switches to another language, some hybrid. He slides off the bar stool and walks about as he speaks, gesturing with his free hand. Ioana cocks an ear and gives me an impish smile.

"That's dialect!" she whispers.

Fritz is speaking louder now, his mild manner fraying. He sounds annoyed, even angry. After a few more exchanges he snaps the red phone back on its cradle and scowls at the walls.

"What happened?" asks Ioana, perched on the sofa. Fritz folds his arms, gazing down at his shiny black Oxfords. He doesn't look pleased.

"I spoke to that Romanian lady," he mutters. "I asked her a simple question about club membership, twice in German, then in dialect. She didn't have a clue. So I spoke to her German boss. Guess what? That boss doesn't even speak Berndeutsch, not to mention Züri! So I asked her why they rejected my wife, who speaks both. The boss said *it's a tough business*."

He glances across at Ioana and shrugs. The apartment is silent until Ioana starts to laugh, rocking gently back and forth on the sofa, as if suddenly liberated from her misery.

"A tough business?" she howls, delighted. "No, it's Capra Vecinului!"

Fritz and I exchange a puzzled look. So Ioana explains about Capra Vecinului – *The Neighbour's Goat.* It's an old Romanian fable about a man whose goat dies. That night he prays for the neighbour's goat to die as well.

Haide, fă pişu!

I'm stressed. Jack is arriving from Italy. "In four days time!" he tells me down a crackly line. He needs an apartment on a five month lease, downtown. I'm in a Bucharest supermarket and he's in a Tuscany tavern, drinking my health on Friday night. "Seems you're my fixer!" he adds, nonchalantly. "I hope you can do it. One bedroom, please! Anything you want me to bring?" I feel like saying *yes please, a magician.* What are my chances of finding the right place at the right price, by Tuesday?

A woman comes down the aisle in a chequered fur coat of different colours – black, maroon and green. *What animal has green fur?* She's pushing a squeaky steel trolley containing a young boy, chin on his knees, enjoying the ride. The boy is old enough to know better. Then again, so is Jack. So much for my quiet weekend – he's due in four days and his budget won't last long in Romanian hotels.

At the checkout I grab a couple of newspapers. At home I scan the ads, feet up with a glass of runny yoghurt and a chunk of bread. But the rental prices are insane. I check the map on my wall, in search of inspiration. Why does life have to be a rush? I walk to the window and look out through leafless trees. Above a nearby shop, I see a sign: *Apartments for Renting.*

Saturday starts cold but sunny. Petru from the rental agency wears a big smile and a little black cap. He has shiny red cheeks, square pants, stout boots and a dark blue coat of padded cotton. He looks like he should be pumping coal on the Shanghai Express, circa 1930. Instead, he's my guide to *several highly-desirable residences.* Soon, we're inspecting the first.

The flat is bare and cold. Not even a chair, just dusty corners, paper clips and last year's calendar askew on a damp wall. I have a feeling there has been a misunderstanding.

"Excellent location! It was an office," explains Petru, proudly showing me around.

"And what is it now?" I ask, following behind.

"Now?" says Petru.

"I said furnished, remember?"

"Furnished?" says Petru.

On our way to the next one, he tells me how he enjoyed living in London, *so much.* He used to work there *for an NGO.* I ask him which one. He avoids the issue, so I ask him again. It turns out Petru was a dishwasher in a café. I tell him I did the same in France, for a year. He's interested and we swap tales. Then I tell him that a café is not really an NGO. He agrees and tells me it was more of a job agency. You paid your money, then a bit more, and then you got a job. What you didn't get was a work visa. But he knows Bayswater *like the back of my head.*

The next flat is better, but still not right. This time the landlady turns up, doused in *Poison*, her powdered double chin buried in the luxurious fur of a dead animal. The flat is well-furnished but full of mouldy secrets. The landlady is full of *don't-do-this*, *don't-do-that*. I thank her and leave.

Petru trots after me down the stairs, asking why. Two down, three to go.

An hour later and I'm almost frozen from the wintry chill. But we're at the final address on Petru's list. City centre, sixth floor, so far so good. The corridor smells a bit off, but he's got a twinkle in his eye as he turns the key in the polished oak door. We enter the flat. It's perfect: fully-furnished, clean rooms, good heating and a great view. We crunch some numbers.

"I'll take it," I say, scarcely believing my luck.

"I knew it! I knew you'd like this one best!" Petru replies, beaming, "The neighbours are all professional people and the elevator never jams!"

Given Petru's talents as a clairvoyant and my two aching feet, I'm tempted to ask why we came here last. But life is full of mysteries – such as estate agents who try to let the worst, first. I sign some photocopied forms and return home, where I cook an omelette, thinking it over. Petru saw me coming, sure as eggs. But he should've listened and saved us both an Arctic hike.

On Tuesday Jack arrives and moves in, thrilled to bits.

"Nice one, Mike!" he says, handing me a bottle of something I won't drink until the anti-freeze runs out.

A few days later, he invites me round to toast his new abode. We take the elevator that never jams, sharing it with a little old Romanian lady who wears a beige Burberry scarf.

Cradling a six-pack of beer, Jack turns towards me, with a puzzled expression.

"By the way, what does *hide-a-fur-pea-shoe* mean?" he asks.

The old lady's eyes swivel in her skull as she gives us a disapproving glance. I edge sideways to Jack and explain as best I can.

"It's what parents say to a kid: *Haide, fă pişu!* It means *Come on, do a pee!* Why do you ask?"

Jack sucks his teeth, looks a bit concerned.

"Because late last night," he explains, "My neighbour kept whispering it over and over, outside my door. So I looked through the peephole. He was walking up and down the corridor in his slippers, talking to a little dog on a lead."

Bubbles

I'm puzzled. Why doesn't someone complain? The noise is deafening. Isn't Sunday afternoon a time for peace and quiet, so people can relax after a hard week at work?

"Not in Berceni," says Mihai, my retired Romanian friend. He flashes a toothy grin as we watch from the cramped balcony of his tiny flat in blue-collar Bucharest.

In the wide dusty courtyard below, tough-looking young guys in polyester tracksuits lounge around an old Dacia. The car has a dragon painted on the bonnet and an aerofoil on the boot, presumably to stop it taking off at 60 mph. The vehicle's doors are wide open and a powerful sound system is pumping turbo-folk music at a volume likely to induce nosebleeds in small children and angina attacks in the elderly. The singer on the CD sounds like he jammed his fingers in a door. But the gang of lads listening to it couldn't care less about that, or about the neighbours, who have to listen to this for hours on end. They seem to live in a bubble. They scowl and spit, laugh and joke, stub out cigarettes then light more. One lad paws at a doe-eyed girl in a tight top and short skirt. It looks like a sultry play by Tennessee Williams, with no interval.

"Can't you call the cops?" I suggest.

Mihai hoots with laughter as he unplugs a small bottle of clear plum brandy.

"Relax, drink this!" he suggests, "and I'll tell you about cops!"

I move away from the balcony, my ears ringing.

"But it's so anti-social, so unfair," I continue, jerking my thumb.

Mihai laughs again, as if to say *what would you know about unfair?*

He places his little bottle on a shelf stacked with old newspapers, porcelain dogs, an ancient electric kettle and a faded photo of Romania's football team. He leads me into his tiny sitting room. His wife Rodica is perched on the old sofa, giggling at the TV and popping sunflower seeds faster than a parrot. Between mouthfuls, she mutters answers to the quiz show.

"Last week," says Mihai, as we settle into armchairs, "my old neighbour was washing his car with a bucket and sponge. Then the cops turned up and told him *it's against the law.* Apparently, these days, we have to go to a car wash. But that costs, right? So, naturally, the old guy starts answering back. So the cops fined him on the spot, a tenth of his monthly pension. Can you believe it, an old guy who survives on beans and potatoes? Anyway, let's watch this."

Mihai boots up the volume on the TV until the windows rattle. Added to the noise from outside, I feel like my vital organs are about to liquefy.

When the quiz show finishes, Rodica serves us tasty soup followed by baked fish, smoked aubergine salad, boiled eggs, pickled cucumbers, *mămăligă* corn porridge and fried potatoes. Mihai thrusts small glasses of hooch at me and we toast great Romanian footballers, great Romanian writers and Lieutenant Columbo – it seems Mihai is a big fan of the one-eyed detective. Later his wife brings us a tray of sweet cakes and a big steaming pot of strong coffee. By the time I leave, I'm stuffed like a French goose, and buzzing.

Next morning en route to the office, I spot soapy water pooling on the pavement outside a Ministry building. I track shiny purple bubbles to a line of big black VIP cars, all dripping wet.

A chauffeur in a suit is carefully sponging them down, from a red plastic bucket. I tell him *that's not allowed, it's against the law*. He looks up at me like I'm the village idiot.

Someone in the Village

I'm delighted. We're going to the countryside – *mergem la ţară* – Lumi, her Italian husband Marco and me. We'll be visiting her folks, taking supplies, they've invited me along.

After an early breakfast I help pack the red Lancia hatchback with domestic essentials: soap powder, bleach, huge plastic sacks of dried cat food, a metal rack for laundry, sticks of salami, shampoo, sugar, ground coffee and empty plastic bottles for bringing back home-made wine. The boot is soon stuffed like a cowboy's chuck wagon. By ten o'clock, we're off. Marco drives fast but safely. The countryside whizzes past and we arrive in good time.

Lumi's parents live in a tiny hamlet of rutted tracks and ramshackle cottages. They waddle out to guide us into their driveway, like two garden gnomes in thick woolly jumpers and hats. Their faces are nut brown. Lumi's mother Anna kisses me on the cheek. Her skin is smooth as marble, her eyes clear and bright. She unloads the goodies like a kid at Christmas. Lumi's Dad Mitu smells of booze and nicotine. He wears battered Nike Air Jordans and doesn't say much. He just smiles, shuffles around and grunts appreciation. Lumi gives him a caustic look.

Mitu beckons me out back, wants to give me a tour. The yard is full of animals: sarcastic geese, nervous turkeys, ducks, cats, skinny dogs, gossiping pigeons and dozens of hens. A huge wooden barrel squats near a fence, stained purple from grapes. It looks like a giant plum. An ancient bathtub sits nearby, encrusted with grey cement. In a small outhouse Mitu proudly shows me a big wicker basket full of big brown eggs. Across the yard, an old blind woman sits outside a neat white cottage. She hunches forward on the veranda, elbows on her knees, all dressed in black. As we pass by she tilts her head to listen, tracking our movement.

"Who's the old lady?" I ask.

But Mitu doesn't answer. She's not his problem. Later, I find out she's his mother-in-law.

Anna makes a superb lunch of deep-fried sheep's cheese, fried eggs, *mămăligă* corn porridge, succulent home-grown tomatoes, spicy pickles and crusty bread. She serves it on their terrace, under a canopy of vines. The sun dapples our plates as we eat. Birdsong echoes through high trees all around. It's rural bliss, like sitting in the Garden of Eden. Mitu pours big glasses of purple wine, boasting how he had a good vintage last year. As we eat, a skeletal dog watches us from the garden of a crumbling grey shack. It stares through a broken wire fence with keen eyes, tongue hanging out. Anna explains why.

"That neighbour's gone away. She's been a bit odd since her husband fell off the tractor. Secretive and always trotting off to hospital, for tests she doesn't need. Cruel too, she leaves her dog chained up with no food. So we feed it. First time, she was gone for two weeks. We only found out after three days of dog howling. Now she's gone again. We have no idea when she'll be back."

The dog watches, as if listening. It seems malnourished but its coat is thick and heavy around the neck. It has long splayed legs like a colt's. I click my tongue and it cocks an ear.

"Looks like a wolf," I suggest, jokingly.

"Could be related," Lumi tells me. I give her a dubious look. "I'm serious," she continues. "We're not far from Transylvania, plenty of 'em up there."

I check to see if Lumi has vampire fangs. Her dad giggles and plonks another two-litre plastic bottle of purple wine on the table.

"*Château Mitu*," says Marco, filling the glasses. Mitu grins to himself. After lunch Anna clears our plates and disappears into her kitchen, where pots dangle. She returns with a plastic bowl of yellow maize flour and pokes it through the broken wire fence for the dog next door. It licks at the dish ravenously, its snout soon covered in the coarse yellow powder, like a clown's.

I catch Lumi's eye and point at the left-over scraps of meat and fish in the bowls on the table.

"Needs some protein too," I suggest. Lumi shrugs, as if to say it's beyond her control.

"Needs what?" asks Anna, glancing up at me.

So I tell her about muscle mass, healthy diet. But Anna doesn't seem to be listening. She fusses around the table, stacking dishes. Mitu blinks at me over his glass.

"Forget it, Mike," sighs Lumi. "Country dogs eat maize flour, if they're lucky."

I watch the dog through the fence. Its bowl is empty. The dog stands back, ready for more.

Across the table, Lumi no longer looks happy or excited. She looks fed up, as if the joy of coming to the countryside is starting to wear off. Marco asks Mitu about football. I get the feeling he's trying to change the subject, like he knows the right buttons to press to avoid family trouble.

"Anna, maize is OK for chickens," I suggest. "But dogs need more."

"If you feed a dog too much," replies Anna, "it gets rabies."

She removes the plates with the scraps of meat and fish. The skinny dog watches her through the fence with keen, puzzled eyes. It looks like it wants to offer a second opinion.

"Says who?" I ask.

But once again, Anna is not listening. She waddles back into her kitchen, waving away the flies. Mitu lights a cigarette and answers on her behalf.

"Someone in the village," he says, puffing smoke.

I point at the last plate on our table. It contains two fried eggs – leftovers.

"Why not give those to the dog?" I ask.

Mitu doesn't answer. It's not his problem. Anna reappears, wiping her hands on a ragged cloth. "No, we can't do that," she says, "I'll give them to the hens."

Summer of Love

"Want to come?" asks Marco over coffee in Lumi's village. He waves a ticket for a night out in Constanţa: *Summer of Love.* "Lumi wants to stay here with her folks," he adds, "but I want to hear DJ Pasha, how about you?"

"I'm in," I reply, reaching for the ticket. What better than a long night bobbing to the beat, with smiley souls on the Black Sea?

We depart early evening in his Lancia and arrive at the seaside a couple of hours later. We walk along the shore, watching the waves. A few swimmers splash about as wind whistles across the sand. After a bit, we turn back in search of Club Maniac.

The door is guarded by three beefy men in black, flanked by seven stunning women in gold bikinis and high heels. Inside, a warm-up DJ is skilfully weaving tunes. But the atmosphere is stiff – nobody dances. Morose looking guys and tanned girls line the shiny walls or crouch around low tables, staring at new arrivals. Marco and I back out. A haughty bikini babe stamps my wrist with a logo. Out front, a teenager in holey jeans yells into his phone, something about a lost ticket. Another kid roots in a furry purse on his arm. Marco and I sit on the sea wall to chat.

The hours pass in Chinese whispers: *DJ Pasha will play soon, definitely by two.* After a rubber omelette and several cokes in a café, we hear a roar and squeeze back inside Club Maniac, at 3 am. It is jammed on both levels, maybe a thousand guests. But the mood is not warm and inviting like a rave – it's still edgy, showy, more like a *Playboy* party crossed with a Las Vegas wrestling extravaganza. Marco seems to sense it too. He shrugs at me under flashing lights: *Whatever!*

Onstage, a good-looking young Romanian guy – famous-for-being-famous – grabs a microphone and bawls a cheesy welcome to *DJ-Pasha-from-the-UK*, who glances up from his decks, waving. The heavy beats pound us into submission. We find our dancing feet. But something is wrong: soon we see that tonight is not about *love*, it's about having the sharpest elbows, the biggest biceps or the deepest cleavage. Before long, the thrill is gone. I follow Marco, inching upstairs.

The Chill-Out Zone is a balcony where plush sofas cost $500 for the evening. The red one is occupied by a sweating slob in his fifties who snorts like a bull walrus and thrusts aside anyone blocking his view – he is certainly chilling. We return to the dance floor, where someone pokes me hard in the back. I turn and a drunken woman pushes me aside with a *fuck you* pout. She takes my space and starts thrusting Tyson arms over her head, hips like a minibus. I leave.

Outside, a teenager vomits into stubbly grass. It's 5 am. Two lithe young ladies in sunglasses and mini skirts tumble from a sleek car, followed by a short bald dude in a tight black vest and gold chains. He waddles into the club, nudging doormen like big buddies. I walk with Marco to the beach, yawning at a rising sun. Huge waves hammer the shore as we stroll barefoot in bubbles. Young guys in jeans run and dive into the heavy surf. It seems rather a bad idea.

Sure enough, when we get back to Lumi's village, the *tragic death by drowning of eight people in Constanţa* gets a brief mention on the evening news. We sip our soup and wonder.

Mystery Train

I can hardly believe my eyes. It seems so modern. The steel body shines with immaculate paintwork; the windows are wide, slightly convex and made of thick tinted glass. Rugged steps and chrome hand rails gleam invitingly in the early morning sun. I board the train in Bucharest's main railway station.

Inside, the pale grey vinyl floor is surprisingly free of chewing gum. I choose a seat by the window. It feels well-designed, covered in bright blue fabric, firm but comfortable. I watch passengers walking along the platform outside. Soon the carriage begins to fill up.

A middle-aged woman sits down opposite me, hair frosted like a cake, fingers dripping gold. She roots through a big leather bag, pulling out a bottle of juice and a glossy magazine. She pops some chewing gum in her mouth and takes a moment to inspect me over her elegant designer specs. I can almost hear the wheels grinding in her head: *he's not Romanian.* It must be my green rubbery skin, bulbous purple eye and furry antennae. She smiles briefly. It could be a welcome, or pity.

The train pulls out of Gara de Nord, slowly picking up speed, *clicketty-clack*. I watch as dilapidated apartment blocks sail past; a kid leans perilously from a rusty balcony, picking his nose. A skinny woman in a headscarf pins sagging sheets to a washing line. It still looks like Romania out there, apart from the snarling yellow diggers and new roads with sleek cars. But in here, I feel I've shot forward in time. I fold my arms and marvel. It's a bit of a mystery, progress.

Not so long ago, the carriages were small, dusty and cramped. The seats were old and sunken, with rusty springs poking through worn velour. The passengers would insist on closed windows, always. If you opened one, they made faces, muttered about draughts, flu, catching their death. Then they'd stand up and slap it shut, fixing you with a cold stare, as if to say *forget it.* Strange then, that some trains had doors that hung open for hours. Like that unforgettable overnight trip from Transylvania to Bucharest, when snow flurried down the corridor until dawn – I slept fitfully in my coat and caught viral pneumonia.

Music from overhead speakers wakes me from my reveries. Soon it is unbearably loud, and hardly ambient: the bass pumps, the singer raps about being a *tough mutha.* It's a din. Nobody else seems to mind. But I do. I can't relax, I can't read, I can hardly think. After half an hour of brain damage, I catch the eye of the Ticket Collector and ask him to reduce the volume.

"You're supposed to enjoy it," he replies, gawping at me with glassy eyes.

"I appreciate the thought," I reply, "but not the volume. Please?"

He shuffles off and soon the din from the speakers subsides by a few decibels. The middle-aged lady sitting opposite me leans forward, stinking of *Chanel No. 5.*

"Good idea", she tells me, chewing gum. "Are you American?"

"No," I reply.

"Australian?"

I shake my head and she moves onto more interesting things. She spends the next half-hour explaining how her beautiful daughter married a wealthy Lebanese businessman who prefers her not to mix with *inferior people.* They have three cars, a pool and lots of shoes. She's got photos.

"Look, in Paris, I've been there!" she adds in a loud, tinkling voice. "La Tour Eiffel! Two and a half million rivets, did you know?"

I've riveted. Eventually, our train pulls into a station and she rises to leave. She doesn't say goodbye. She sticks her chewing gum under her seat and waddles quickly away down the aisle. In her absence, the place smells like a perfume shop, the sort where you can hardly breathe. I stand up to open a window.

From a nearby seat, a wizened old chap with a big moustache stares at me in horror.

Baby

Nicole looks just the same. Quick smile, high cheekbones, hair swept back in a loose, luxurious bun. Her dark Romanian eyes sparkle with intelligence, mischief. She still has a distinctive way of dressing, like she's off to meet the Wizard of Oz. Cute red shoes, white socks, bold skirt. We hug and kiss, laughing. Is it really three years? I'm eager for the gossip, from India.

"Let's go onto the terrace," she says, ruefully, "bit too crowded in here."

I follow Nicole across the room, glancing around her parent's huge old apartment. Suitcases are strewn in the corners, their lids open like giant clams; baby clothes hang from radiators, a pack of Pampers stuffed under a cushion. There's a wobbly pile of shiny books with little pink tickets sticking out, as if someone has been busy reading up. An empty milk carton lies on the ironing board, spout gaping like a hungry duck. It's quite a mess, but I don't ask why.

Nicole leads me through French windows into bright sunshine. The terrace is spacious with ancient earthenware plant pots coated in green velvety lichen. It commands a superb view of downtown Bucharest. She offers me an old wooden seat near the rusty barbecue.

"A madhouse, yes?" she laughs, quietly. I shrug, not wanting to agree. She rolls her eyes. "It's Juliette, my younger sister. She was always the baby. My parents are too soft."

Her voice tails off as she gazes across the city. I wait, sensing there's more to come.

"She had Marius two weeks ago, her first kid," continues Nicole. "Two days later her husband Dragoş rented out their flat across town. They moved here and asked my Mum to look after the baby. Then they went back to work. Juliette left a list of *guidelines*, as if she knows."

Nicole chuckles but looks tired of the subject, so I ask about India. She updates me and talks about her hard-working, permanently-stressed British husband. "We're lucky in some ways," sighs Nicole, "protected by his diplomatic status. But whenever Pakistan heats up, things get tricky. Worse than when you were around, trust me!" I nod in sympathy.

"Look," says Nicole, pointing over the terrace to the street below. A large middle-aged woman slowly edges a pram through busy traffic, her head rotating like an owl on espresso.

"There's my Mum, been to the doctor with Marius."

I ask why. Nicole leans against the iron railings, whose rusted curlicues seem to offer a glimpse of Bucharest as *Little Paris*.

"Because he almost died of starvation," she replies. She glances up and catches me staring. "Juliette read every baby book under the sun. But she learns by rote, like a parrot. She doesn't compare, analyze or think for herself. Dragoş is the same. Educated but dim, both of them."

"Starvation?" I ask, incredulous. Nicole nods, folding her arms. "Juliette said *breast milk only.* She got that from those damn baby books. Plus, her Romanian doctors told her *if you love your baby, breast milk only*."

"But isn't breast milk good for a new baby?" I ask, lost now.

"Of course, but what if the mother produces too little? That's why Marius was howling the house down and didn't look well. I told Juliette to fetch a doctor, she refused. So I called a paediatrician. He took one look and said *this child is dying*. He put Marius on a drip. The kid had hypernatremic dehydration and had lost thirty percent of his birth weight. So much for baby books!"

"Oh," I reply, stunned.

"And guess what, Juliette blamed Mum!"

"Why?" I ask, surprised.

"Good question. But that's Juliette, can't see the wood for the trees."

When Nicole's Mum joins us later on the sunny terrace, she's carrying Marius. He's sleeping like a baby.

Why?

"He walked from Russia to Romania?" I ask, incredulous. I can hardly believe my ears. My friend Vlad nods, hands deep in his black jacket. I look again at the corpse laid out before us. The dead man is about 80 years old, or rather he was. Today he has tissues stuffed up his nose and a cheap coffin for a bed, lined with knobbly brown candles that flicker in the gloom.

"Why did he do that?" I ask.

Vlad explains that in 1945, his Grandpa – *Tataia* – had been a Romanian prisoner of war in Soviet Russia. The only way home was to walk.

"He said it took him a few months and he ate rotten dog meat to stay alive," adds Vlad. "He loved dogs after that, tamed wild ones here in the village. Some stayed, some ran off. But he always said *they'll come back,* and guess what, they usually did, for food probably." Vlad shakes his head and wipes dribbling tears.

A few hours later, after singing and prayers, Tataia's funeral procession winds through the village. Fifty people walk behind the horse and cart, including his blind widow, Mamaia, bent double. Some of the other old ladies are sobbing to the sky, most of the men train their eyes on the muddy track. At each rutted crossroads, the priest stops the procession for prayers, chanting in a mournful voice. As we move on, men toss coins and sweets for a gang of kids.

"Why are they doing that?" I ask.

"It's a tradition," Vlad whispers. "The money pays for Tataia to enter the realm of the dead."

And presumably, the sweets are a modern bonus. Vlad's dark eyes are ringed red, his nose is leaking. Clouds hang low in the sky, the countryside is flat on all sides and a bitter wind howls across the endless farmland. I try to imagine how far it must be, from here to Russia.

Tataia is lowered into the earth, carefully wrapped in a fine shroud of transparent white gauze. Somebody produces a bottle and pours a little dark red wine into the grave. It spatters on the white shroud like blood. Tataia appears to have been shot by the Mafia. Wooden planks are arranged on top of his coffin, then soil. A weeping woman hugs an old stone cross nearby.

On the slow walk home, some old ladies gossip in low voices about *the stranger.* So I ask Vlad what they're saying about me. He moves closer to cock an ear and returns half-smiling.

"Actually, they're not talking about you. They're discussing some old guy who came over from another village, a few kilometres away."

"Oh," I reply, feeling somewhat disappointed.

"But by the way Mike, to these folks you're not exactly a stranger. . . "

I half-smile back, puzzled but touched. It's nice to be part of a community, even if it is just for one sad day.

". . . you're an extra-terrestrial," concludes Vlad, without a hint of irony.

Back at the cottage, the mood lightens as we sit down to a feast. Tataia's widow, Mamaia, sits at the head of the table, hunched in black with a brown face and firm nose. Her unseeing eyes glisten like hailstones. The long trellis table groans under plates of roast meat, fried fish, fluffy yellow *mămăligă,* pungent goat's cheese, bread and endless bottle of wine. A black dog curls at our feet. I feed it some titbits.

"Does the dog have a name?" I ask. Vlad inquires around the table and then replies:

"No, Tataia didn't have a dog when he died. It's probably a stray."

The dog is completely black. I nudge Vlad in the ribs.

"Dressed for a funeral, what do you think?" I ask, with a smile.

Vlad glances under the table. The dog's eyes shine back at us in the fading light. Vlad laughs and pours more wine.

"Could be," he admits.

Vlad and I return to the village a few months later, with supplies for his grandma. He roots in her old kitchen cupboard and shows me a tatty document with some figures typed on it. He points to the final column: *25 lei.*

"Mamaia's pension," he explains, shaking his head. "Seven euros per month after a life spent slaving in fields and factories. How are old people supposed to survive here?"

He chats with Mamaia for a bit then invites me next door to meet her old neighbour.

"Come and hear this," he says.

The toothless farmer next door is named Mihai. He sits in a cramped kitchen with religious icons stuck to the uneven, whitewashed walls. He fidgets with a worn penknife as he tells his tale.

He explains how the stray black dog refused to leave after the funeral feast for Tataia. It slept on Mamaia's step for a week and was always prowling around, getting under his feet.

"So that's why you chased the dog away?" asks Vlad, teasing the story out like a veteran detective. The old farmer lowers his head and nods once, as if finally admitting to a crime. When he looks up at us, he is weeping. Vlad offers a tissue. Mihai blows his ruddy nose and continues.

"Then Tataia appeared to me in a dream. But he was very angry. He shouted at me, saying: *Mihai, why did you chase my dog? I sent it to look after my widow!*"

Vlad turns to me. But I'm staring at the old farmer, spooked.

"Why did I do such a thing?" moans Mihai, wiping his eyes. Vlad grips his leathery wrist.

"Don't worry Mihai, the dog will come back. They always do, remember?"

The toothless old farmer nods again, gazing down at his battered flip-flops.

Why Not?

Twelve years ago? Hard to believe it. The music still sounds as fresh today as it did back in 1995. I sit on my friend's sofa, staring at the speakers of his audio system, entranced. The bass is clear and locked tight with the drums. The guitar soars, raucous yet controlled. The singer seems to be in a world of his own, a dreamy voice spinning tales of puppets and trees and endless love. Now he's sitting next to me. Adrian passes me a photograph. We are both in it, looking young and happy.

"Why Not?" he says, and he's right. That was the name of his band. I look closer. The picture is grainy but captures five young guys in lively spirits on a snowy day in Sibiu. We are all walking across Liar's Bridge. We had met a few months before, and anything seemed possible.

"Remember?" asks Adrian, leaning on my shoulder.

I remember the rock festival in Craiova, where I saw them onstage for the first time. It was a hot day. They played mid-afternoon, way down the bill. I was sitting in the damp theatre listening to their songs with all those catchy, melodic choruses. That guitarist knew a trick or two. The drummer and bassist were solid. Upfront, the singer cavorted like a man possessed, whirling like a dervish. It was their first live concert and I was hooked. The festival was full of sweaty, overweight guys in black leather and red bandanas, churning out heavy-metal. But this band was much more original. They sang rock that sounded like folk, and folk that sounded like rock. But what got me, most of all, was that special *something:* even though their music was as raw as 1950s blues, as playful as '60s pop and as powerful as '70s rock, they didn't sound like anyone else. That's the key, the magic dust. You can't buy it or fake it.

After the show, I had asked the local promoter for an introduction. I remember standing in the shadows at the side of the stage, watching him approach the wide-eyed singer with my request. But the singer shook his head. He turned in slow circles, folded his arms. He seemed troubled. He wore a big baggy white shirt and tight pants, like Jim Morrison. I remember being puzzled. *Maybe he doesn't like foreigners?* But after a moment he walked towards me, head down, hands-in-pockets. He said *hello* and told me his name was Adrian. Then he said something that made the hairs on my neck stand up, and sealed our friendship forever.

"Last night I prayed for an Englishman to help my band."

We stared at each other in disbelief, as if wondering who should speak next. Me, I guess.

"That's why I'm here," I replied. "I want to manage you."

"Why not?" he replied and we shook hands on destiny, or something. How could we fail?

A month later the band stayed with me in Bucharest and recorded a demo tape in a studio called CAT. Behind a big mixing desk sat the in-house producer – veteran Romanian rocker, Adrian Ordeanu. He knew his stuff, miking the drums just right to get a nice crisp *whack* from the snare and a big fat *thump* from the kick. On the dirty blues numbers the guitar sounded like glass breaking, but on the ballads it sounded as gentle as wind chimes – the perfect combination. The bass throbbed like an underground train. Throughout the two-day recording session I made sure the boys had enough snacks and juice. The final tape was music to our ears.

"Pretty good," said Ordeanu, shaking our hands as we left, exhausted. "And good luck."

Over the next few weeks I trawled the nightclubs of Bucharest, trying to generate interest in a band nobody had heard of, chatting with bar managers and promoters. They seemed reluctant at first. Transylvania was not considered very hip in those days. The real action was down here, in the sophisticated South. But when I finally got the club guys to sit and listen for five minutes, they seemed intrigued. I could tell from their expressions. They had never heard anything like it.

"From where, you said?" asked a puzzled-looking dude in a smoky office. Posters of rock gods and sexy babes on Harleys plastered the walls, but he had eyes only for his battered stereo.

"Sibiu," I replied, "although I found them in Craiova."

"You certainly found something," he answered, opening a big diary of green leatherette. Sure enough, concerts followed, including one show at the hippest joint in town – *Lăptăria lui Enache*, Enache's Milk Bar – upstairs in the National Theatre. The band got a decent response from a bemused but openminded crowd. Other venues were less friendly – notably a student cellar – where some of the slick city kids booed and yelled *go back to the hills!* Afterwards, Adrian had grabbed my arm, ashen-faced and angry. He began drilling me with questions: "Why were they so rude?"

"Why not?" I replied, urging him to toughen up. I told him about the time a London crowd threw lighted cigarettes at me onstage. "If you can't stand the heat, Adrian?," I asked.

The highlight of our collaboration was an open-air show in Buzau. Adrian was on top form and the sky rang with wild applause. Our bass player was sick and I filled his shoes. I hadn't played live for years, but once that big fat drum starts, you pick up where you left off.

Next, we mimed a slot on TV for a youth programme. The teenagers in the audience seemed to love it, the glamorous young presenter too. We were on our way to the top. A week later, Adrian phoned to say a legend of Romania's jazz-blues scene, pianist Andrei Colompar, had somehow heard the tape from CAT studio. He probably got it from Adrian Ordeanu, the producer.

"Guess what Colompar told me, Mike?"

"No idea. *Get a better manager*, maybe?"

"No!" yelled Adrian, laughing. "He said we have *gold in our hands!*"

"That's very nice," I replied. "Ask him how we transfer it to a bank account."

The word was out, and spreading. Before long, national radio invited Why Not? for a live Q&A – a chance to impress the whole country. But the young female presenter was rude and spent most of the show flirting with her technician, while the band's songs were being broadcast. During the interview, she seemed more concerned to show off her English by interviewing me, than to talk to the young Romanian guys who wrote and played the songs. All in all, it was a disappointment.

Afterwards, in the gloomy cavernous corridors of Radio Romania, I asked her why she had not been more professional, and paid more attention to the songs and the musicians.

"I can evaluate music and talk at the same time," she giggled, "that's why I'm a journalist, you see." I told her I was a BBC radio trainer and had never heard such nonsense. She looked surprised then fired back: "It's a special skill." Unique more like.

Back then, that night on Radio Romania had seemed like a lost opportunity, our rapid rise blocked by a bimbo. For some reason, it marked a watershed. The band imploded within months. To me it seemed like a tragedy, the end of a dream. I had been convinced that with a lot of hard work and a little bit of luck, these four lads from Sibiu could show Romania there was more to modern music than long hair, ragged black jeans and ten minute guitar solos. Undoubtedly, I was on some kind of Brian Epstein trip. Most band managers are.

Today, Adrian and I laugh about it, sitting in his front room and listening to the old songs. They still sound perfect. Soft rain plays a mysterious melody on the windows as we talk about his new life. He got married, had a kid and found work as a technician in a theatre in Sibiu, running the sound-and-light desk for all the shows. It gave him a bug for drama, a natural progression for a front-man.

"So I enrolled at college," he says, "four years in Tîrgu Mureş, theatre classes every weekend. It allowed me to keep my job. Hard work with all that travelling, but I graduated."

Now he works as an actor, puppeteer and clown. He shows me a photo. He's dressed in baggy silk pants of yellow and blue, with a spotty shirt and a funny little hat. He's standing on a chair, making faces at a gang of kids. They watch with big eyes, tiny hands clasped in wonder.

"This is what you were meant to do. It's your vocation," I tell him. Adrian shrugs.

"Whatever it is, I love it."

Then he updates me on the rest of the guys. Carmen the bass player has a kid. Julian the guitarist broke Adrian's heart when the other three started a new band in secret. But it flopped. Without their wobbly-voiced leader upfront, the old chemistry had apparently fizzled out. Adrian got over it. Julian got divorced and went to teach English in Japan.

"I hope he took his guitar," I say. The one I brought from Liverpool, as a gift. "And what about Dan the drummer, what's he up to?"

"Working in IT. And that rude radio presenter, I wonder what she's doing?" asks Adrian, sipping a beer.

"Probably running some radio station, made it big," I reply. He looks peeved at that.

"You know," he mutters, "we had *gold in our hands*. I sometimes wonder why we didn't. . ."

"Didn't what?" I ask.

Adrian is gazing through the window, onto a yard of wet cobbles.

"Make it big," he replies, in a quiet voice.

"But you did!" I tell him. "Be proud of what you achieved!"

Adrian shrugs, looks again at the old photo of five young guys on a bridge, and says:

"Yeah, why not?"

Money to Burn

The speeding car hits the cat. The driver didn't see or didn't care. The cat spins sideways with a high-pitched cry, legs splayed. It lands in the gutter a few yards ahead of me and tries to run, but cannot. The car roars past me. The driver glances in his mirror but doesn't stop.

The cat wobbles in the gutter then slumps down as I approach. It tries to meow, but makes no sound. Blood trickles on dusty fur. I pick it up carefully, muttering pointless words of comfort. It is small, filthy and skinny. No home, probably. I can feel its ribs, like dry macaroni. The back legs hang lifeless, as if broken. The veterinary college is nearby. *Maybe if I'm quick?*

Five minutes later I'm walking down a shiny, silent corridor, in search of the emergency room. Inside, I find two women and a young guy wearing white cotton tops, like medics. I introduce myself and pull the mashed cat from my rucksack, which now stinks of shit. The vet and her two trainees move quickly, keen to take over.

The vet examines the cat with a troubled look, clicking her tongue. Her two students crouch at the stainless steel table to watch. The cat stares with pale green eyes, as if in shock.

"You must fill in a form and pay 20 lei for hospital tax," the vet tells me. Then her young trainee guy points to an X-ray machine behind me and adds:

"Plus an extra 50 lei, so we can scan for internal injuries. OK?"

I agree to the deal and he leads me to an admin office, where I sign forms and open my wallet. But it contains only 15 lei. The young guy frowns and then suggests an ATM outside, as if he doesn't quite believe me. So, we walk and talk. His English is good and he seems a nice lad.

"I graduate next year, I plan to start a small clinic," he confides. "But first, I'll work for an experienced vet. That way I'll learn. I don't want to kill animals later on, right?" He laughs and produces a slim cigarette. "Got a light?"

By the time we return, the cat has a shaved tummy and a drip in its paw.

"What are the chances?" I ask.

The female vet shrugs. She doesn't look too optimistic.

"With two broken legs? Fifty-fifty, I reckon. If she survives tonight, I'll operate and fix her, no extra charge. She's a street-cat and you did a good thing."

I leave the vet college and hurry uptown for a session with my dentist. When I explain why I'm late, he snorts with derision:

"All for a stupid cat? Next you'll be saving worms. What about people starving in Africa?"

I ask him if he has no compassion for animals.

"I hate cats," he says, flatly.

Next day, I return to the vet college to check on progress. A clerk tells me the cat died overnight. She hands me a receipt for the 70 lei I paid.

"Sorry, we did our best."

Later at home, I get a call from someone at the vet college who asks for *the British guy*. He seems concerned and says:

"You must come back and pay 150 lei, so I can put the cat in the incinerator."

I do some sums in my head. 50? I tell him I already paid 70 lei and it's not even my cat.

"Mister," he replies quietly, "If you don't pay me to burn your dead cat, I have no idea what will happen to it."

After a few moments, I tell him: "Neither have I."

Then I hang up.

Democracy

The Vice-President raps his hairy knuckles on the table and barks a command.

"Quiet, please, our esteemed President will address the meeting!"

The chatting residents fall silent. There are sixteen of us sitting on chairs in the cramped corridor on the second floor of our block. Sunshine glazes the windows.

The President rises from his seat and adjusts his red tie, tugs the cuffs of his baggy suit. He has black bushy eyebrows, a drinker's nose and yellow teeth. He begins to read from a document. The back of it is covered in florid handwriting – probably his speech.

"Dear neighbours, welcome to the block meeting for 2007. Since we are now a democracy, you will all have a chance to speak later. Today we vote on many key issues, such as buying a hosepipe and tools for the garden. Not to mention next year's committee. So with your permission, I shall begin. First, may I say that we had very, very good results last year."

From the next seat, my neighbour Lumi shoots me a bored grin, eyes sparkling as if to say: *Results? He looks after a residential block, he's not the manager of a company!*

The President rambles on, occasionally glancing at us over his specs, just to make sure we're all paying attention.

I do my best, but after a while I get bored and look through the cracked window to my right. In the yard below, Tina, the old cleaner, is bent double, sweeping rubbish. Lumi is watching her too. We exchange a brief look. *What a job.*

The President announces the first vote: pay rises for himself, for Administrator Vlaicu and his bossy wife. Nobody objects. Except Lumi, who asks:

"What about Tina?"

The VP looks concerned and does some quick sums with a pencil.

"I suppose we could give her 10 lei," he admits. He's young and fresh-faced, no doubt keen to seem reasonable. But Vlaicu the Administrator seems about to lay an egg.

"Not Tina!" he snaps, perched on the edge of his seat. His voice booms down the corridor. Tina glances up from the yard, as if she heard it. Vlaicu's chest is heaving.

"By the time she pays tax, it won't be worth her while!" he adds. A brief silence follows, while the residents mull it over. But then someone asks:

"So, why did you get a rise?"

Silent descends once more. Vlaicu glares around the residents like he could put thumbscrews on us all. But the President seems to sense the wind of political change and waves a hand, saying:

"Give Tina 20 percent, who cares."

Vlaicu slumps back in his chair, steaming in defeat.

"Now let's vote on the water meters," suggests the VP, jowls a-tremble.

"Why? We don't need to buy them," hisses Vlaicu.

With his clear skin, baby blue eyes and collegiate mop of silvery hair, he might pass for a genial academic. A lady in a baggy tracksuit nods enthusiastically and chips in:

"Our esteemed Administrator is correct! They're a trick invented by someone in the West, who thinks we're stupid." She flashes me a dark look, as if I might know who. I raise my hand. The President spots it and seems to be amused by my presence, but he encourages me to speak.

"Let's hear it, English."

"Meters are not a scam," I suggest. "They will help everyone to pay their due, and they can prevent errors." Before anyone can respond, clicking heels on the stairs signal a late arrival.

A frail woman in a spongy brown coat pokes her chin round the open doorway, like a cat checking for dogs. She spots Vlaicu, who rolls his eyes as if to say *oh no*. She speaks in a firm voice: "If you lot are electing presidents, please elect one who's reliable. Not someone who's never around and you have to wait a week to find him. That's all." Then her head vanishes, like a puppet's yanked from behind by hands unseen.

"Thank you, Mrs. Dumitrescu," sighs Vlaicu. His loyal lieutenant in the baggy tracksuit stands up and waddles to the open door, then she screams down the landing:

"Go to hell! Every time you wash your balcony, dirty water drips onto mine!"

The President calls for order and explains how water meters work. He admits he's in favour of the idea, even if it is a capitalist one. He mentions how the meters are well-made and cannot be tampered with, because they all have *cocks and nipples*. Everyone laughs, especially the old guys aged ninety-ten, who sit shuddering red-faced in their black funeral suits.

The next vote is about whether or not to buy a new light bulb for the elevator. Some residents say they don't mind standing in the dark *if it saves money.* But the President overrules them, explaining that we live in a modern democracy, plus he lives on the first floor and must use the lift several times a day.

"Besides," he adds, "the Turk on the top floor offered to donate a lamp from his shop."

Then we discuss smelly bathrooms.

"Mine stinks," complains Lumi, "I even considered selling my flat."

Vlaicu looks up, baby blue eyes twinkling.

"So why don't you?" he asks, sarcastically. A middle-aged man in a wide tie tells Vlaicu not to be rude. Lumi replies that she just wants to fix the problem, not move out.

"I simply want to find out why the plumbing smells so bad," she continues. "And, as you all know, this is not the first time I've asked."

The President busies himself shuffling papers. The VP murmurs to Vlaicu, who nods and replies: "It's because the Chinese renovated their apartment."

A few heads turn, as if checking whether our Chinese residents are present. They are not. Vlaicu's bossy wife waves a finger and mutters darkly: "They have gadgets in their kitchen."

Next, someone asks why the rubbish chute gets blocked every week.

"Because of that Dumitrescu on the third floor," grunts Vlaicu, tapping the VP's notepad, as if he wants it written down. Nobody objects and Mr. Dumitrescu isn't here to protest. The VP scribbles the verdict, pen clutched in his podgy fist.

By now, the air is stale and mouths are yawning, even though it's only 11 am. Then Vlaicu makes a surprise announcement: he may resign from the Committee.

"Even though I am passionate about my job, I'm ill. I take costly pills imported from abroad and need time to go to resorts. But I don't want people saying I'm skiving…"

The woman in the baggy tracksuit looks aghast, running bony fingers through her hennaed hair and urging him to stay on. Other residents look somewhat less concerned. Vlaicu shrugs and says: "Thank you all for your support, I'll think about it." Then an old guy in a baseball hat complains about dog hair. Vlaicu yells "I agree! From that huge dog! It lives with the German guy, yes?" A smiley lady with gold teeth intervenes: "But what a beauty!"

The President then announces *new candidates* for next year's Committee and reads out the five names of those currently serving. A quiet man in a faded sweater shakes his head: "We need new blood. I propose Lumi." Others agree. But Vlaicu objects, saying: "Lumi plans to sell her flat and probably won't be around, because of the Chinese." Lumi shrugs, indifferent.

There's a final hurried vote. Some residents complain they don't understand.

"Just vote, vote!" urges the President, checking his watch. Then the quiet man in the sweater asks: "And what about that graffiti, scratched in the elevator?"

Silence falls. Heads turn, smiles and frowns are exchanged.

"Why, what does it say?" asks Vlaicu.

"*Suck me, Vlaicu,*" says the old guy in the sweater. Administrator Vlaicu doesn't flinch. The President waves a hand and says:

"Who cares, that's democracy."

Brotherly Love

I'm shocked. Tanti Aneta lies in the hospital bed, propped on pillows, looking a shadow of her former self. She was always a bit frail, but today she looks like a skeleton that just woke up. The good news is that the stroke was not severe, and her partial paralysis is fading.

"At least I can speak now," she adds, slurring her words. "And I'll be out soon, then I can get back to Gheorghe, he needs me." I squeeze her hand, which feels cool to the touch.

"You need to rest," I reply. "Isn't there anyone else, who lives locally?"

Tanti Aneta tries to smile, but seems sad.

"Virgil is already circling," she adds, mysteriously.

"Who?" I ask, puzzled.

"My brother-in-law," she replies. "Remember *Jaws*? That's Virgil."

"I didn't even know Gheorghe had a brother," I say, bemused.

"It's a long story," says Tanti Aneta. And then she tells me.

Next time we meet, a month later, she's perched on the battered sofa in her small apartment in Brăila, gazing at a polished sideboard full of tiny porcelain dogs, every breed you can think of. These days the place smells of urine, and I know why. From the next room, I catch the sound of her husband Gheorghe wheezing. After a few moments, he shuffles through the doorway, his frail hands shaking violently as if he's seen a ghost or had an electric shock. But no, his motor skills are impaired due to Parkinson's Disease.

Uncle Gheorghe is on his way to the toilet. Incontinence is one of the symptoms. That's why the flat smells of pee. A stocky guy walks behind him, guiding with a firm hand and kind words. It's Virgil, Tanti Aneta's brother-in-law, the alleged shark.

Virgil is about the same height as Gheorghe and has the same square head, like a shoe box covered with hair. I warm my palms against a radiator, wondering about family secrets.

Over the twelve years I've known Tanti Aneta, I've never heard of Virgil, never met him and never seen a photo. Until last month, when she had her stroke and I discovered that he lives 300 meters away and has big plans. According to Tanti Aneta, Virgil wants Gheorghe to sell the apartment and hand over the money. He knows his brother is losing his marbles. Seems he's also a bully who thinks women should be seen and not heard, especially his sister-in-law – which is presumably why Tanti Aneta has never mentioned him until I went to the hospital.

The sound of peeing echoes down the hall. Virgil reappears and paces around the room, like he's in charge. Tanti Aneta stares into space, like he's not there.

"This is tragic," says Virgil, head in hand.

Actually, he's not a bad actor. It's like Oscar Night: *And the winner for Best Brother is . . .*

"Virgil, pardon me for asking," I begin, "but why do you want them to sell up?"

"Because I'm concerned," he replies, loosening the collar of his lumberjack shirt.

"About what?" barks Aneta, finally breaking her silence, "Parkinson's Disease? We can manage, we always manage!"

But Virgil sucks his teeth and glances down the hall towards the loo, like he has doubts.

"Not according to my dear brother," he replies. "I've just had a word with him."

By now Tanti Aneta seems close to tears, but she's not done yet.

"About what? He's been ill for years!" she snaps. "Where were you?!"

Virgil ignores her taunts and looks straight at me as if to say *see what I mean?*

Gheorghe emerges from the bathroom, dragging his feet in maroon slippers, head bobbing up and down like a plastic dog in the back of a car. Virgil tells him to sit. Gheorghe slides his bony bum onto a dining chair, gasping for breath. He looks troubled by the loud voices.

"Virgil's right," he stammers. "You can't cope, Aneta, not after your stroke. You're on your way out, we both are. So we should sell the flat, give Virgil the money and move into his spare room. He will take care of us."

"What?" wails Tanti Aneta, "that's not what we…"

But Gheorghe raises a waxy finger and cuts her off.

"Be quiet, I should've divorced you years ago, like my brother says."

Tanti Aneta gawks at me, speechless. Virgil rubs a firm finger along polished wood and glances around the flat, thinking.

Welcome to the EU!

"You don't have a *television*?" asks Denis, glancing around my sitting room, wide-eyed with wonder. I shake my head. He checks the kitchen and bedroom, just in case. He looks deeply troubled. "Incredible," he adds. "But don't worry, we do! So that's another reason you'll visit for New Year! Europe, here we come!" He lunges forward and kisses me hard on the cheek, like we're Mafiosi. Then he's gone.

Sure enough, on December 31, the TV dominates the sitting room in Denis' small apartment. The volume is at full-blast. Grinning celebrities poke fun at one another, and most channels seem to show young Romanian men pretending to be middle-aged women, or middle-aged Romanian women pretending to be disco babes. *Mutton dressed as lamb.*

Denis and his wife Raluca sit on the sofa, chuckling at the screen. Their two young kids – Mariana and Ovidiu – lounge around, pawing at Christmas toys that seem to have already lost their magic spell. The dining table is stacked high with tasty food and drink, and we are all doing our best to reduce the pile and increase our waistlines. After all, it's New Year's Eve.

By eleven, the kids have grey rings under their eyes and look rather fed up. I ask if they've got a pack of playing cards and they nod, curious. I ask their Mum if I can take them into the next room and she agrees, so we decamp as a trio.

We squat on the floor below a huge, blank TV screen, playing Cheat. Little Ovidiu squeals when Mariana guesses it wrong and thumps the air when he guesses right. Before long, their faces are red with excitement and they're dragging out dolls and soldiers and asking me *which one do you prefer.* Next we're all drawing silly cartoons of each other on paper with felt pens.

The door flies open and Raluca strides in.

"Put the TV on!" she yells. Before I can reply, she prods a button and the huge screen kicks into life above us. On-screen, a group of well-dressed, middle-aged Romanians are sitting around a long dining table flanked by faux Greek statues, chatting away and poking at designer food. They look rich and bored. The camera tracks their every move. Raluca beams at me.

"What?" I ask.

She points at the screen.

"He's a rich old guy who married a young woman. Now she's pregnant!"

Puzzled, I glance back at the TV.

"And?" I ask. Raluca frowns at me, evidently disappointed.

"And this is their TV show!" she giggles. "It's awful but just see how they live!"

Then she perches on a bed, watching the television. The two kids kneel up and drop their crayons, entranced. Denis appears, carrying on his shoulder a huge boom-box which thunders an old disco tune. He grabs me by the arm and tells me every Boney M track has a special meaning for him. I am starting to feel as if we are all characters in a play by Ionescu. Denis yells at me:

"*Brown Girl in the Ring!* I was in the army. We put chilli up a dog's arse. That was fun."

At midnight we watch fireworks on TV. Dennis produces a box of rockets and lights one at the kitchen window. It zooms off into the night like a shooting star. The kids jump for joy.

"These are illegal!" laughs Denis, as sparks fly. He gives rockets to Mariana and Ovidiu, and ignites their fuses with a cigarette lighter. It looks like an accident waiting to happen.

"Welcome to the EU!" he says, sloshed.

"I'm British, we're already in it," I reply, waving a sparkler, trying to write my name.

At nine the next morning, we finally go to bed. I sleep on the sofa. We wake at noon, to the sound of loud cracks. Curious, I amble to the window and look down into the street.

Men dressed in traditional white costumes are walking up and down, waving long rope whips and turning a hurdy-gurdy for money. Neighbours throw coins and notes. So we do it too.

"It's a tradition," explains Raluca, wrapped in a bathrobe, tossing down a few lei.

"Why?" I ask, intrigued.

"No idea," replies Denis, sipping coffee. Then he grabs the remote. "Let's watch TV."

Number Three

Young Sorin looks like he's carrying the worries of the world. I wonder why. He slouches at his PC, chin in hand, poking at the keyboard. His fingertip is stained yellow from nicotine. I edge closer on the sofa.

"What's the problem, mate?"

It sounds corny, the kind of thing an adult should not say. But Sorin doesn't seem to mind.

"Girls," he sighs.

I should've known. Sixteen is never an easy age. Seems all his friends have steady girls. He's had two, but they weren't nice. He's desperate to meet number three.

"Have you spoken to Mamaia?" I suggest. Sorin stares at me in disbelief.

"Mamaia? She's over eighty and totally blind," he grunts, "what does she know?"

I beckon him with a finger.

"You'd be surprised. Let's go."

We find Mamaia sitting in her tiny kitchen, listening to her radio. As usual, she's wearing several layers of clothing and knitted slippers. A bright headscarf frames her tanned face, deep lines etched into smooth skin. Her eyeballs are shrivelled and coated with a patina of pale grey.

“How many husbands did you have, Mamaia?” I ask. She turns to the sound of my voice.

“Three, why?” she fires back, turning down the radio with a knobbly finger. I sit on a hard wooden chair and explain that Sorin has *romantic trouble.*

“Of course he does!” cackles Mamaia, with a gummy grin.

“Can you advise him?” I ask. Sorin looks interested for a change. But Mamaia just shakes her head, hands on bony knees.

“No, I can’t.” I nudge Sorin in the ribs, as if to say *you try.*

“Three husbands – how come?” he asks.

Mamaia sucks a sunflower seed then says: “First time, it was love. I was 18. Gabriel was older, a bit of a drinker. Two months later he went to war. Never came back, never saw his son Mihai – he’s your grandpa, by the way.”

Sorin grins and says “I know that.”

“You don’t know much,” cackles Mamaia. “In ‘46, a Gypsy came to my door, claiming he’d been with Gabriel when he died. Told me *Your Gabriel said if I ever make it back, I can have his wedding suit.* So that was that. You want advice, young Sorin? I’ll give you advice.”

Young Sorin glances at me, all ears, as Mamaia moves onto Husband Number 2:

“I first met Petru after the war. Eventually we got married and I had my second child – that’s your Tanti Raluca, by the way. But Petru died of TB – he’d spent months sleeping on wet ground in a prison camp. That’s the Russians for you, *beasts* he called them.”

I watch, trying to guess what’s going on inside Sorin’s adolescent head. Suddenly, war is more than severed limbs on his PC.

"I've lost my sunflower seeds," mutters Mamaia, groping around. Sorin finds her packet and presses it back into her wide, waxy palms. "And Number 3?" he asks. Mamaia flashes a couple of stubby grey teeth, like tiny gravestones. "Indeed," she sighs. "Number three."

Sirens wail across town as she explains that her third husband was a POW who walked home from Odessa, Russia.

"Silviu came to our village as a shepherd. Every summer he lived out in the fields in a hole in the ground, under a roof of grass and branches, very clean and cool it was in there. He knew how to make the best cheese. He'd get sacks of fresh vegetables from the villagers for grazing their sheep. We got friendly. He proposed. After I said *yes,* he told me he already had two young kids but would leave his other woman and bring them to me. I was a little surprised but what could I say? I had two little ones of my own and nobody to provide for us, so..."

She pauses and reaches around the wobbly old table until she finds her glass of water.

"We never had kids together, but we had a nice life. We had a cherry tree, a pear tree, and a big vineyard. He didn't drink much, but he was a bit of a ladies' man I think. Best mates with all the widows!"

Mamaia giggles like a schoolgirl, as if proud of his exploits.

"He gave up his shepherd life and got a job as night guard at the CAP."

"What's CAP? "asks Sorin. Mamaia chuckles to herself.

"Cooperativa Agricolă de Producţie," she replies, "He used to guard the grain. Him and his big sheepdogs. He was a hard worker, my Silviu. Until he got sick and died. Cigarettes – they wrecked his circulation."

Sorin glances at his yellowed fingertips and slides his right hand under his knee.

"So Mamaia," I ask, "What do you think Sorin should do, about his romantic trouble?"

"No idea. What's her name?" asks Mamaia.

"That's just it," replies Sorin, sadly. "I've had two, but I'm still looking for the right one."

Mamaia sucks her sunflower seeds. She seems to be thinking it over.

"If you meet a flirt, don't worry," she says. "They'll grow out of it. But if you meet a drinker, forget it. They never will."

Sorin sighs and looks at me across Mamaia's kitchen.

"Is that it?" he asks, scratching his head and sounding disappointed. Mamaia reaches for his right hand, rubbing her fingers gently over his nicotine fingertips. Sorin's mouth drops open.

"Number three will be best of all," she mutters. "But stop smoking."

Fairy Tale

They look nice, all these women walking around clutching flowers. A gawky teenager in jeans, grinning and sniffing at a single rose; slick ladies in smart suits, high heels clicking as they emerge from offices carrying elaborate bouquets; a happy, grey-haired grandmother with a bunch of snowdrops. There's something sweet and even girlish about them all, as if touched by the magic of spring. Sure enough, when I arrive home I find my neighbour Lumi in the lobby of our block holding five pink tulips.

"Happy Women's Day," I say, feeling guilty, wishing they were from me. "What have you got planned for tonight? Marco taking you out for dinner?"

Lumi fishes in her handbag and pulls out a ticket for *Swan Lake*. She waves it in front of me, as if teasing. "Hubby's working late," she replies. "Want to come to the ballet?"

Two hours later we settle into our seats, five rows from the stage at the National Opera House. The place is crammed with people, all dressed to kill: handsome young dudes in dark suits escorting skinny women in glittering sheaths; chatty mums in deep furs; tiny girls prancing around in their best frocks; even an ex-President of Romania, grinning as usual, flanked by his bodyguard. The house lights dim. A hush descends over the audience. Any second now, we'll be transported in time and space to a fairyland, where a lonely Prince will fall for a beautiful swan.

But not yet; instead, the spotlight falls on a large guy, aged around 45, wearing a three-piece suit and a smile, as if he knows something we don't. He stands centre-stage, his sideburns sculpted into raffish points like some 18th century ladies' man. His pony tail looks like it came off the back of a horse – long and frizzy, reaching down the middle of his back. He talks for twenty minutes about how *we all appreciate women* and *this is their special day*. He seems to savour the attention. A little girl in the next row tugs at her dad's sleeve as if to ask *where are the swans?*

The big guy introduces a famous former ballerina and a couple of VIPs, including the UN Ambassador to Romania, who wears a spectacular red gown and reads a speech about how she plans to dedicate herself to *improving women's rights, ending forced labour, stopping rape and all other forms of violence against women.* Then she reads a special message from Ban Ki-moon, her big boss. Everyone claps and little girls bring flowers on stage. In the front row, some of the handsome guys in suits are busy checking their phones, prodding buttons and reading texts.

When it finally gets going, the ballet is first-class. The Prince leaps and dives, the prima ballerina flutters and glides like a beautiful swan. A trio of tiny girls trot down to the front for a better look. The orchestra zips through Tchaikovsky's pounding melodies. It's a stunning show.

In the pause, there's a fuss upstairs in one of the gilded galleries. A young blonde woman weeps and is comforted by a group of worried looking ushers. The gossip spreads fast. Lumi listens in, then turns to me to explain.

"Apparently some guy punched her in the face and ran off."

A gong booms majestically throughout the building, for the next bit of the fairy tale.

Domnul!

What a taxi! What a car! Dacia Logan: modern, air-conditioned, a smooth ride and apparently they're not too expensive. Friendly driver too, asking me *how's business* and offering keen insight on football, China, Iraq, you name it. If this is the new Romania, I'm staying.

I glance at the meter. The decimal point seems to be in the wrong place, but with this new lei currency, who knows. After a ten-minute trip, he drops me off.

"Sixty-five, please, *Domnul!*" he says. I do some quick sums in my head, converting into dollars, then euros. It seems rather more than usual. "Do you mean 6.5 lei?" I ask, still confused. But he shakes his head and points at the meter: "Sixty-five, *Domnul*." Something's not right.

"Twenty euros?" I reply, "For a couple of miles? Are you kidding?"

I laugh and climb out of the taxi, offering ten lei from my wallet. But he refuses to accept it.

"*Domnul!* Sixty-five!" he barks. "Look outside, on my door. Check the tariff!"

"I checked it before I got in," I reply. But now his self-assurance makes me wonder.

"Check again," he mutters.

I look at the outside of his door. My eyes pop. His tariff is not 1.4 lei per kilometre, but 7.4. The first digit is painted so it resembles '1' at first glance. Clever.

"This is a scam," I reply and put the ten lei on the empty passenger seat. The driver leaps out of the car and we square up in the busy street. Headlights flash and horns honk as we yell at each other. He calls me a *tight-fisted western jerk*. I tell him I am not paying €20 for a short ride. He reaches into his cab, grabs the intercom and barks:

"I've got a situation here."

I ask him for his VAT number; I tell him I'm going to the cops. At first, he seems not to care. But eventually we compromise on 40 lei, about €12. He slams his door and drives, shouting *idiotule!*

In the lobby of my block, I find my neighbour Lumi, checking her mailbox. I tell her what happened. She smiles sympathetically and tells me there's a new breed of unscrupulous taxi drivers, with shiny cars and exorbitant rates, who hang around look for gullible foreigners.

"They found one," I reply. "I can't believe I fell for it."

"Always check the door," she says. "And take the metro if you can."

Next day, I'm weaving through the crowds, watching the bustling road, trying to find a cab. I'm late and too far from the nearest metro. A smiling driver opens the door of his gleaming yellow Logan, like Aladdin with his cave. I check the door, just in case.

"*Domnul!*" he shouts. But I shake my head. He looks peeved and yells "Why not?" I point at the 7.4 on his door and reply "Too much." He glares and hisses at me: "So take a tram!"

Instead, I grab a bus, squeezing aboard as it lurches into honking traffic. It's packed with passengers and the July sun hammers on the roof, cooking us alive. I slide my ticket into the stamping machine then stash my wallet back into my old briefcase.

A young, obese man with black hair and dark eyes wriggles through the packed aisle towards me, puffing and panting like he's auditioning for the role of Fat Guy in some comedy film. He says something to me and grins. But it's no joke. It's hot today, 40 degrees centigrade at least. He watches as I reply the best I can. When he turns away, I catch a whiff of last night's garlic on his breath.

I lower my head to look out of the window. Huge grey apartment blocks line the busy road, with furniture showrooms and banks and offices tucked below. I remember when these were stuck in contractual limbo, all empty, half-built, like the ruins of some ancient civilisation. *Tempus fugit.*

The sweaty fat guy wriggles closer until he's standing directly in front of me, mopping his brow and staring into my face like we're about to get married. From below, I feel a tug on the strap of my briefcase as it snags against a seat. I pull it up tight to my tummy, just to be safe.

Sirens wail and two motorbikes flash past outside, followed by three shiny black cars with black windows and little flags on their bonnets: VIPs in a desperate hurry to serve the people.

The fat guy is still huffing and puffing and wriggling inches from my face. I feel like telling him: *Hey, you got the part.* As the bus slows, someone squeezes past to get off. I feel another tug at my briefcase. That's twice. *Like someone is up to something.* Or maybe I'm imagining it? I pull my bag closer. The fat man grins at me, sweat trickling down his nose. The poor fellow looks like he's due for a heart attack. I tell him *it's hot.* He rolls his eyes. *You bet.*

I get off the bus fifteen minutes later, my shirt wet and sticky. As I walk to my apartment, I stop for a cold drink from the corner shop. I open my briefcase. My wallet is gone.

"The fat guy robbed me," I mumble to myself, wondering how he did it. Then I realize his exertions and smiles were a cover. What magicians call *misdirection*. He was one clever thief. Now he's got my UK driver's license, my credit cards, some cash and a photo I cannot replace. I stand among bottle tops in the gutter, watching the bus disappear down the dusty road.

"*Domnul!*" cries a friendly male voice from somewhere behind me.

Stuck

I'm curious. I look closer at the email in my Inbox, wondering. I know the name, but can't place the face, until I click on the attachment. In the photo she has sent, Adela looks older and wiser but still flashes her trademark laconic smile, as if there's more to life than a pretty face. She has a handsome husband standing behind her and a cute little girl on her knee. Her message reads: *I heard you're back in Romania? Come visit! Check our website, I got promoted!*

The website turns out to be Under Construction, but her invitation is genuine.

I few weeks later I arrive in Constanţa. Adela is keen to show off her home – bigger than where she used to live with her grandmother and a feisty cat. She shows me a big sofa and says *your bed.* Her daughter Tasha is a pocketful of giggles, watching me like I just landed from Mars.

Cornel arrives home from work and seems like a nice husband, more helpful around the house than most Romanian guys I know. He's about 30 years old with short hair, shirt and tie, cool frameless specs and an endless supply of daft jokes. He's easy going, seems to light up the house with his innocent love of life. He brings tea and biscuits and says he has a question for me.

"Do you prefer hunting or fishing?"

"I don't like either," I reply.

He seems disappointed, but not for long.

"I've heard all about how Adela learned journalism from you in Bucharest," he continues. "But what are you doing now?"

"Good question," I reply, "Short-term stuff, mostly. And yourself?"

Cornel reveals that he works in the Administration section of a local food factory.

"Most days it's boring, just stats and charts," he adds, but then he brightens up. "But actually, today was quite good!" He seems to be hoping I'll follow up, so I oblige.

"Why was that?"

Cornel reaches into a smart leather briefcase and slides out a single sheet of white graph paper, with nothing on it. Then he turns it over, smiling to himself. On the reverse, on the plain side, there is a detailed, hand-drawn picture of a pistol.

"Because I did that, in three hours," he says. I look at the drawing, then at Cornel, then at Adela, who sighs and turns away. I have the impression she's almost as confused as I am.

"What is it?" I ask.

Cornel looks puzzled for a moment.

"It's a Luger," he replies.

Over dinner, Cornel wants to discuss my past: what it was like growing up in England with no communism. But I want to discuss his future: what it might be like growing up in Romania, with capitalism; working hard and moving on. Cornel blinks as if I'm talking Chinese.

"You don't understand," he replies. "My job is awful. There's nothing to do all day. I just pretend to work. I'm stuck in a hole, as you say in England."

"I think you mean *rut*," I suggest, "*stuck in a rut*."

"Yes, one of those," says Cornel. "And I can't get out. Not unless I do exams and…"

But he doesn't finish the sentence. Presumably he'd prefer to draw guns.

Next day, I meet Adela at her radio station. It's been refurbished since my last visit and is buzzing, a hive of activity now. It has a smart reception and a flash new logo. She shows me her office, all neat and tidy, stacked with files. She takes three phone calls in five minutes. I sit in the corner, watching her work, I'm proud to see how far she's come, my ambitious student. She's doing well, leading all these busy bees. But I'm puzzled about her and Cornel.

Later that evening, we're out strolling along a quiet dirt road, in a hilly area above the town. It's getting dark and we've had a nice walk. Little Tasha skips about squealing as Cornel chases her, whooping like an Apache. Adela and I lag behind, chatting over old times.

"Seems like yesterday," I suggest.

"Do you remember when…" she asks, and we're off again, howling with laughter.

Darkness soon envelops our group. Cornel flips on a torch and announces:

"Witches used to live in this bit." Adela tells him not to frighten the tourists. But he insists. A few moments later, his torch beam picks out a fat frog, with spots on its tummy.

"Sent by the witches?" I suggest. Cornel warns me not to joke, lest the frog cast a spell.

I walk alone into darkness, staring up in silent wonder at the stars. I don't think I have ever seen so many. Suddenly the world disappears from below my feet. I feel myself falling. I have no idea why. I land with a painful crack, in a jumble of twisted limbs. It hurts. I'm on my back, staring up at glittering black sky, in agony.

"What happened?" I moan.

Somewhere above, I can hear Adela laughing so hard she is almost crying. Then I hear Cornel hooting like a madman. He's staring down at me, hands on his knees, rocking.

"You fell into a hole!" he yells, fighting back the tears.

As my head clears, I see where I am. It's some kind of pit, at least one meter deep. Even worse, I can't get out. I'm stuck.

Nice sofa

"Change the locks," I suggest, "the next time they go out. Then, when they come back, you just tell them *no more access to my apartment until you pay your rent.*"

But Maria clearly thinks this would be a step too far. She looks dejected, confused.

"Locks cost money," she replies.

To be fair, she's in a spot, aged sixty-plus, with a sick husband. They rented out their town flat several years previously and moved to the sticks. Now they live off the land and have $50 per month from their tenants back in Ploieşti, at least in theory. But they stopped paying rent six months ago.

"Plus, they already changed the locks to keep me out. Any other ideas?" asks Maria. She sits back on my sofa, testing the cushions with the palm of her hand. She seems to approve.

"Did you phone them?" I suggest, pouring tea. She glances around my flat and asks why I've got so many lamps. I tell her I like the effect.

"Do you like the bills?" she asks, raising her cup. She's funny, my neighbour's Mum. But this isn't. Plus, I don't mind being hospitable when she forgets her key, but I'm not her stooge.

"Maria, did you phone them?" I ask again.

"My tenants can't afford a mobile phone," she says. "And they *always work late*, as if."

"What's late got to do with it?"

"They know the last bus to our village leaves Ploieşti at 5pm, so I can't wait. Clever, eh?"

Sirens wail down the busy street below my block. I walk to the window, trying to think of a way for Maria to outwit her foxy tenants. It reminds me of some scallywags I once knew in Britain. They stopped paying rent, and when they secretly moved out, they stole a beautiful Victorian fireplace. But I don't think Maria wants to hear about that. She just wants a solution.

On the blocks opposite mine, I spot a large yellow banner draped over a balcony: *Apartments for Sale.* It takes a while for the penny to drop. But eventually, it does.

"That's it! Look!"

"What?" asks Maria. She joins me at the window and I point to the yellow banner.

"Sell the flat! That would solve your tenant problem! Put the money in a deposit and you'll earn a lot more interest than rent! The longer you keep the cash, the bigger it grows!"

"I'll think about it," says Maria, looking doubtful. She checks her watch and gets her hat.

"I think Dan will be home now. Thank you for your hospitality. You have a very nice sofa."

Then she shuffles down the corridor in her winter coat, towards my neighbour's apartment.

When spring arrives, Dan from next door tells me that his parents finally sold their rundown flat in Ploieşti for $25,000.

"The buyer was an old friend from the same block," Dan explains, "who needed to find space for his extended family: *win-win*, as you say?"

"Great!" I reply, "And what about those foxy tenants?"

Dan shakes his head in despair.

"They kept delaying, begging to stay longer so they could find a new place. The new owner got fed up and booted them out, seems there was quite a screaming match in the yard."

I suddenly feel a twinge of guilt. I try to imagine how it would feel to get booted onto the street. Was it my fault, the wise-guy with big ideas? Dan seems to read my mind.

"Don't worry", he says. "When our friend eventually got inside, he discovered that my folks' flat was decorated like a five-star hotel: plasma TV, big mirrors, cocktail bar, everything!"

I stare at him.

"Nice sofa too," he adds. "So Mum grabbed that, instead of rent."

"And is she happy now?" I ask.

"Of course," replies Dan. "She says it's even better than yours."

Tranquillity

Is every city like this? I'm standing on my balcony, looking down onto a busy car park where a space costs €8 per day. The car alarms are beeping, howling and wailing. It spreads like a virus down the street. Nobody seems to mind. Young men and women stand around in business suits, smoking and chatting in the sunshine. Maybe they're already deaf. But who owns all these noisy cars? Presumably people who live or work here. Presumably most of them know how their car alarm sounds. Presumably, they couldn't care less if it beeps, howls and wails all day or night. As a result, my neighbourhood sounds like a video arcade, 24/7. Is every city like this? I walk back inside my apartment and sit at my laptop. After a few minutes surfing, I find the answer: no.

In New York, there is a pressure group called *Noise Off: The Citizens Coalition against Noise Pollution.* Members cite car alarms high on their political hit-list. They stage silent demos – hundreds of residents marching on City Hall. Plus, they know their rights: laws dating to 1992 require alarms in New York to be turned off after three minutes, or the car owner can be fined up to $700. I gaze at the screen of my laptop, wondering how to organize a demonstration. *No way.*

After a few more clicks of my mouse, I'm surfing a site about noise pollution back home in the UK. There, it seems local councils can break into and silence a car after 30 minutes, and the owner has to pay for any costs.

Next click: Russia, where even Moscow City Council has banned car alarms because *'people cannot protect their property at the cost of sacrificing the peace and health of others'*. Something to do with sudden surges of adrenaline in our blood, it seems. Another website claims 30 Italian cities have banned car alarms. Who knows?

I move away from my desk, while yet another high-pitched tone reverberates around my block. It sounds as if Bucharest is being invaded by UFOs. It's time to escape, time for some air.

So I walk downtown, taking the backstreets, where there is less traffic. Young kids play happily under stumpy trees and dogs pad about sniffing for scraps. The noise soon fades and after a few twists and turns, I find an old monastery. It's late afternoon and the place seems like an oasis of tranquility. I find a wall to sit on and gaze up at the fine red brickwork, wondering who built it and when. Two monks dressed in long black robes and bushy black beards wander around, chatting. It seems like a nice life, away from the hustle and bustle: *just you and your mates and God.* It's around 4.45 in the afternoon when the clacking starts.

It sounds like someone is tapping wooden sticks together. After a few moments, I notice a little old woman walking towards the monastery. She wears a brown coat and pink bonnet. Next comes a middle-aged man with a walking stick, stiff up one side of his body. Soon there are more and more people, coming to pray. As they enter the church, they make the sign of the cross, heads bowed.

The clacking grows louder and faster. Soon the rickety noise is echoing off the walls of the modern blocks around the old monastery. A bell booms from the tower, clanging its deep sonorous voice across grey metal rooftops. It's a wonderful sound, mystical and ancient.

But before long a mangy street dog decides to pray, howling like a wolf. Somewhere else, another dog barks and soon the blue sky resounds with the moaning and yapping of a dozen hounds, all keen to chase cats in heaven. Soon they're running up and down, barking like crazy and dodging between the dusty trucks, big vans and shiny saloons, all parked in a row.

Then the car alarms start.

Şpagă

It will be the biggest night of my year. I hope. So I should plan ahead, email Sorin, my football buddy. He's a big fan of Steaua Bucharest. He'll help. We'll watch the game together when I get back from Nigeria. That's where I am, tonight. Stuck in Hotel Splendid where room service takes three hours. Lovely people, friendly and smart, but slow? They should call it *Hotel Slug*. Who cares? Not them. Not me! Why? Because my team will play AC Milan in Athens in four weeks and I'll watch it in a bar in Bucharest with my footy buddy. I sit at my laptop and type.

> *Dear Sorin, URGENT! Please reserve a table for two in the sports bar at Hotel Costalot for the Champions League Final, Liverpool V AC Milan. Don't forget! See u there!* ☺ *M.*

I click *Send* and lie in bed watching *Animal Planet*. I fall asleep to the sound of lion cubs squabbling over a dead antelope. Next morning Sorin replies with bad news from the hunt.

> *Sorry Mike, all tables fully booked at the Costalot!* ☹ *Plus I'll be away. S.*

All booked, four weeks ahead? I know Romanians love football, but that's crazy. And no Sorin?

One month later, I land mid-evening at Henri Coandă. It's good to be back. After the chaos and creeping desertification of northern Nigeria, Bucharest feels like New York. My big yellow taxi speeds into town. The friendly driver asks where I've been. I tell him and he gets curious.

"Is it true corruption is a big problem there?"

"Yes, it is."

"How about the people?" he asks.

"Friendly and smart," I reply.

"But have they heard of Romania?" he inquires.

"Yes," I reply. "They asked if gypsies are a problem."

The driver laughs as we drive past Hotel Costalot, the place where I can't get two seats one month ahead.

As usual, the hotel is lit up like a spaceship. Shiny cars with black windows cruise in to dispense chunky guys in tight T's and Aladdin shoes, with their skinny women in lipstick, bias-cut frocks and stilettos. The men waddle into the lobby, rolling their necks like prize-fighters. The women totter behind, jabbing at tiny mobiles. The porters wear little red coats and big white smiles.

Later, I'm sipping tea on the balcony of my flat, watching the lights of Bucharest. I can see Hotel Costalot, a few blocks away. I think about tomorrow night, when the sports bar will be jammed with guys who probably just want to chat, have too many drinks and watch the goals. It doesn't seem fair. When I was a kid, I'd shout for Liverpool from packed terraces while some pensioner peed on the back of my legs through a rolled newspaper. Twice a month, I'd come home with a hoarse voice and stinky jeans. Now this! Maybe I should try again? I could walk there in ten minutes.

I finish my tea, pull on my trainers and take the lift down to the street.

Soon, I glide through the revolving glass doors of Hotel Costalot's glittering lobby and head into the big sports bar where a middle-aged guy in a bow tie is chatting to a busty brunette half his age. She's got one eye on a male gymnast on TV. A young waiter listens to my plea. He's in his early twenties, but looks older with the midnight tan of his trade.

"Tomorrow night?" he replies. "Champions League? Sorry, *Domnul*, all our tables were booked weeks ago!"

I glance around and ask: "What about the bar, can I reserve a stool?"

He looks puzzled and tells me to wait while he goes to check. He hurries away, flapping his spotless linen pinafore like a washerwoman. I hang around enjoying the dubious fruits of globalization: a Brit in Romania watching sport from France on six flat-screen Japanese TVs. How times change! Out of the corner of my eye, I track the young waiter talking to a small woman in a neat black suit, hair in a bun. Her neck cranes sideways, as if she's checking me out. She shakes her head. Sure enough, the waiter returns offering only pointless smiles.

"Sorry, sir, my boss says it is against house policy to reserve bar stools." Then he leans closer and adds: "But take my advice, come at eight and you'll find a stool, no problem!"

"Serious?" I ask, just in case. The waiter gives me a thumbs-up.

"*Trust me, sir*," he says, quietly, "I've worked here long enough to know. Would you care for a drink?"

But I'm already skipping out of the bar, down the marble steps like Fred Astaire, trotting across red carpets and gliding into the balmy night, grinning like a madman. It's a sign. We'll win.

That night I lie awake watching headlights bounce across my bedroom wall. I can't relax. I can't get football off my mind. Police sirens wail up and down, finally lulling me to sleep.

I return to the hotel the next evening, three hours before kick-off, wearing my lucky T-shirt: *'Liverpool FC – UEFA Champions League Winners – 2005'*. But will it help tonight, in 2007? Definitely maybe. I'm floating on hopes and dreams, like a kid at dawn on Christmas Day. The sports bar is half-empty. TV sets hang from the walls, trailing ads for the game. Tables are laden with elegant glasses, cutlery and flowers. Each bears a shiny brass plaque: *Reserved.* I can only smile. Soon those select seats will be occupied by clever, lucky people who planned ahead. I should have known better. Romanians love footy, right? Well, it's only fair, because the early bird gets the worm. No surprises there.

What does surprise me, however, are three shiny brass *Reserved* signs on top of the bar, placed strategically in front of five chrome and leather stools. On the middle stool sits a guy in a blue shirt and tie, sleeves up, his jacket folded on one of the empty places, his crumpled FT on the next, like he's saving places for friends. He gives me a superior look and casually drapes his arms either side of him, as if to say *don't even think about sitting here.* He's a Brit, I can tell: suede brogues, Marks & Sparks suit, untidy hair, tired eyes, pale face, pot belly and 20 Silk Cut.

But something doesn't add up. I order a juice. Then I turn to him and ask:

"Excuse me, did you reserve these stools?"

He grins at me.

"Certainly did mate, two hours ago!" he says. I try my drink, wondering how come.

"Weird," I reply. "I tried 24 hours ago. It's against house policy."

An awkward silence descends, like we're two cowboys playing poker and I just called him a cheat.

"I wouldn't know, mate," he replies. But the tone of his voice suggests that he knows very well, mate. Or at least, he knows more than I do, mate. It's time to find my friendly waiter.

I move away from the bar. I find the waiter under a bank of TVs, testing sports channels with a remote. He recognizes me and says *Milan will win*, then spots my Liverpool T-shirt and adds *well, maybe.* I ask him about house policy. He looks confused. I check his name tag: *Dan*. I tilt my head discreetly at the Brit hogging the bar.

"That guy says he reserved all the stools two hours ago. Now I can't sit down. How come, Dan?"

But Dan doesn't seem to know the answer. He pockets the remote, sucks air and purses his lips like he should have prepared better for his exams.

"Would you like a drink, sir?" he replies, grinning from ear-to-ear like Mickey Mouse.

"No, I'd like to see your boss," I reply, frowning like Daffy Duck.

"Certainly," he says, sliding away on thin ice.

The small lady in black arrives two minutes later, on big heels that click.

"Is there a problem?" she asks, in a tone that suggests there isn't. I start with *house policy.* She nods wisely, because she implements it. But her face changes when I mention Johnny English & The Bar Stools. To me, it sounds like a jazz band. To her, it sounds like insolence.

"Those stools are not reserved," she sighs. Her words hang in the air with her floral perfume. I twist my head to the bar, wondering: am I dreaming? No. I'm wide awake and I-spy-with-my-little-eye three shiny signs sitting on the bar, bold as brass: *Reserved.*

Dan the waiter hovers nearby with a remote. The Brit at the bar is glued to a TV ad for tampons, pretending not to listen.

"Anything else?" asks the little lady with the big job, raising a plucky eyebrow. I feel as if I am ten years old, she runs my school and I shouldn't be in it.

"Not reserved?" I say, pointing helpfully. "Can't you see the brass signs on the bar?"

"Ah," she sighs.

"Ah," I add.

"That gentleman came early," she continues. "The stools are for his friends."

"But you just said they are not reserved. So may I please have one, to watch the game?"

"No, that gentleman asked for them two hours ago."

I get the impression the room is starting to spin. Or maybe it's just my head. I try again.

"*Two* hours ago? I asked you *twenty-four* hours ago!"

"Sir, please, don't raise your voice."

"But you said *no reservations* on bar stools, because of *house policy*! Remember?!"

"Those stools are not reserved," she says, calmly. No irony clouds her blue sky. She's too young. Thirty-five, tops?

She still thinks being a boss is about locking doors, not opening them. She sees me as a threat to be repulsed, not an opportunity to be embraced. All I want is to spend time and money in the bar. But she can't see a solution for me, only a problem for her. She glances at my T-shirt. She probably thinks I'm one of those hooligans from Liverpool. The ones she heard about on the news years ago.

"He is waiting for friends," she says, gazing at me with eyes that do not see. Her face is perfectly symmetrical. She's pretty. Pretty disingenuous.

"How come there's one rule for him, but another rule for me?" I ask. She doesn't answer. The hotel probably flew her to Chicago last month and taught her the joys of management. Somehow, I doubt they mentioned situations like this. Tense moments pass. All around us, TVs boom the latest results from sports events across the globe. But from her? Not a sound.

"Are you deaf?" I ask, louder than I intend. Now I've got her attention. Now she's mad.

"Excuse me, sir! You should not call me deaf! I think you owe me an apology!"

"Me, apologize to you, are you kidding? I think I should talk to your boss."

"I am the boss!"

"No, I mean the boss of the *hotel*."

"This bar is not part of the hotel!" she snaps. Now it's me who's quiet. Moments pass.

"Oh, I see. You just happen to be under the same roof, at the same address?" I ask.

"Yes," she snaps.

I'm not sure what to say next. There's a blur of movement on my right: I turn to see two young guys in suits, buzzing around our barney like flies. One pats me playfully on the arm and says in broken English: "I'm a lawyer, can I help?"

I stare at my arm and reply: "No, you can shut up."

"Sorry," he murmurs. "We're just looking for seats."

His timing is impeccable, but nobody is laughing, least of all me. I'm glaring at the boss. She's glaring at me. Like a pair of ex-lovers.

"Sir?" she mutters.

"Yes?" I reply.

"You owe me an apology".

"No, you owe me a seat!" I howl. I wag a finger at her. Sociologists say it represents a wooden club. I wish. "Something's not right," I add, "and you know it!"

Then I count her sins into the palm of my hand.

"I tried four weeks ago! I tried 24 hours ago! *House policy?* Seems to me it's pretty flexible. Why? Because you think you own this bar. But you don't! Your boss does. And when your boss reads my letter, you'll be sorry you ever met me."

My last resort – sometimes it works. She blinks a few times, thinking it over. Little by little, I sense that something is changing. I have a delicious feeling I've called her bluff: a letter to Head Office from an articulate customer with the moral high ground and a low opinion? That would blot her copybook. Finally, she turns, murmurs to the lurking waiter and stalks off, her shiny heels clicking at me like a terrier in retreat. I watch her go. It seems I've won. Maybe it's a sign. Maybe my team will win.

"Sir?" says the waiter.

"Thank you Dan," I reply and follow him, hoping for the best seat in the house. But he ushers me to a tiny table next to a steaming hamburger grill, with a TV set hanging two metres above my head.

"Is this it?" I ask. Dan backs off quickly.

"I'll bring the menu, sir."

After a few minutes gazing vertically at the TV, I realize I'll soon need a surgical neck brace. Not only that, but the damn burger bar stinks of frying flesh, and as I have not eaten meat for 25 years, I'll probably throw up if I stay here much longer. I sit staring at my shoes. *They're leather. What a hypocrite*. Then I sigh in defeat. It's a sign. I didn't win at all, I lost. My team is going to lose. I've had enough of this place. I wouldn't stay if they paid me. I'll go somewhere else. Some dive, who cares as long as there's a TV? I slide off my stool and leave, meat hissing triumphantly in my ears. On my way out, the nonchalant Brit is ordering another beer, watching Formula 1, getting nicely oiled for the big game. His four stools are still empty; the brass signs still say *Reserved,* except they're not. He sees me coming and avoids eye contact. Good idea.

I'm skulking down the marble staircase when my phone rings. It's my dentist, the one who doesn't like Jews or cats. Nevertheless, he has somehow earned a place in my heart, perhaps because he's the best dentist I ever met and I enjoy his outrageous company. Plus he wants to change. Or so he said. I gaze at my handset, wondering what he wants. I take the call.

"Mike, you know what's happening tonight?" he asks. I hear sirens in the background.

"Of course I know," I bark back. I sound like a hooligan.

"No need to be rude. So where are you watching it? At home, I suppose?"

"I don't have a TV, remember?"

"You don't have a TV?" he asks. I want to remind him that we've had this conversation three hundred times, but I choose silence and continue down marble steps, checking my watch. I've got two hours to find a screen and a seat.

"So where will you watch the game?" asks my dentist.

"That's a good question," I reply. "I have no idea."

"In that case, why don't you join us? Some friends have booked a table in a nice hotel, near your flat. That's why I rang. Sorry for the short notice but…"

I freeze. I cup my free hand over my ear. Bobby Beethoven is tinkling *Moonlight Sonata* on a grand piano in the atrium, wearing a frilly pink shirt and black bow tie. Nice, but too loud.

"Which hotel?" I ask. "Costalot?"

My dentist laughs and says "If you want! See you at nine." Then he hangs up. I lean back against the marble banister, stunned at this fortuitous turn of events. Then I pocket my Nokia and amble downstairs to wait on a deep sofa in the glittering lobby, in a daze. It's a sign, surely? The gods are smiling. Maybe we'll win. If the Wicked Witch of the East lets me back in the bar, that is.

Soon, I'm back upstairs in the sports bar with my dentist, his pretty wife and a gang of their mates, mostly male. We're all sitting around one of the best tables, with half a dozen huge TV screens to choose from. I should be happy. But I'm not. I'm sinking, fast.

Because my team is losing 1-0 after a stupid mistake – we committed a foul, 18 yards out, smack on half-time. AC Milan scored from the free kick. We're in trouble. Unless we can respond like warriors, crush them in part two, just like we did in 2005 from 0-3 down. *The Miracle of Istanbul*, the media said. But tonight in Athens? We've got 45 minutes.

"Cheer up," says the burly, happy Romanian at my side, "and give me your scarf. I'll wear it for good luck." I hear his words but I'm too busy thinking about tactics. Our manager should change the attack, swap some strikers, mix it up and confuse those canny Italians.

"Hey, didn't you hear me?" asks my neighbour. I look up. His name is Marius. He's the guy who booked our table. He has a gold watch. "Give me that!" he says and jabs a brawny finger at the knitted red scarf threading through my hands like prayer beads. I hand him the scarf. He wraps it proudly around his neck, clicks his fingers at a waitress:"Hey, more beer!"

I put my head in my hands and stare at fag ends on the floor. After a morose moment, I look up. Smoke hangs in the air like mountain fog. My dentist's wife is puffing away like a steam train. She's six months pregnant. Her husband catches my eye and gives me a wink. He looks apologetic. He knows where my head is. He's been there. We watched Steaua suffer a similar ordeal months ago. Then it was my turn to console him. That's what friends are for.

"Every dog has its day!" he shouts, "maybe tonight is Milan's turn, after all?"

"Maybe," I reply, with a shrug. I sit up, drink my juice and glance around the sports bar. The place is packed with folks getting plastered and filling their faces with fries and burgers. Some are grinning like maniacs, dressed in black and red for AC Milan. Others wear long faces and red shirts for Liverpool.

45 minutes later, it's all over. I'm catatonic with despair. We lost 2-1. It seems so unfair. We dominated the match, we should've won. What went wrong? Why didn't we use fresh strikers? Life is full of frustrating, unanswered questions. I gaze in misery at six TV screens. On every one, Italian fans are jumping and singing and waving fluorescent emergency flares, oblivious to FIFA's safety ban. They've done it – avenged us for the *Miracle of Istanbul*. Their handsome, muscular heroes dance a jig on green grass, hoisting precious gleaming silver. The European Cup is almost a metre high, the most beautiful trophy in sport. And now it's theirs.

Marius unwraps my precious Liverpool scarf from his neck. He gently passes it back to me like it's the remains of someone I love. He's right. He smiles and gives me a brotherly hug.

"I want a Liverpool shirt for my son," he announces, "and you'll get it."

I try to return his beery smile, despite my turmoil. Marius is pushy but I can't help liking him. He exudes optimism, can-do, will-do. Plus, he did get me a seat. So I reply the best way I can.

"You'll Never Walk Alone."

Marius seems to understand. At times like this, only my club's famous anthem will do. We leave our big table. My dentist wraps a conciliatory arm around me, muttering platitudes. On our way out, I see that the Brit guy is still hogging four empty bar stools for his die-hard footy mates who didn't even turn up. I glance around the room as we head for the exit, curious about those tables reserved weeks in advance. Several are untouched – their plates, napkins and silverware still neatly arranged awaiting guests who presumably decided they didn't like football after all. *You know what, who cares?* It's only the worst night of my year. As we walk down the marble staircase, I have a sneaking feeling I won't be back here for a while. The place has left a bad taste. Maybe it's bad luck. Maybe it's me. Reap what you sow.

"A shirt for my son, don't forget!" slurs Marius, on the stairs. We're best buddies now.

"No problem," I reply. "What size?"

"He's age 14, so how about medium?" he suggests, scratching his head.

"No, I'll get large," I suggest, "So he can grow into it. Liverpool is for life, OK?"

"OK, thanks. I'll tell him. Don't forget."

"My pleasure."

My dentist elbows me in the ribs and yells a jokey good-night. He and his young wife lurch down the steps, keen to get home to see their daughter. I call after them.

"Thanks, you saved my bacon!" My dentist turns and makes a face.

"You don't eat meat!" he yells.

Then they're gone. Marius and I swap numbers, shake hands and promise to stay in touch. His palms are sweaty, his eyes glassy from the booze.

"Thanks for the seat," I say.

"My pleasure," he replies.

"By the way, when did you book the table?" I ask, "Probably ages ago?"

Marius gives me a funny look as he walks towards the big glass revolving doors.

"No," he says, matter-of-factly, over broad shoulders. "I booked it this afternoon."

I follow him behind turning glass, wide-eyed and open-mouthed like a goldfish. Outside, in the car park, I watch in silence while he pats his pockets for his car keys. They dance in his hand like a swarm of bees trying to get up his sleeve. He flicks his wrist in a well-practiced move and a black car starts bleeping and flashing nearby.

"This afternoon?" I reply, wondering if we inhabit the same universe. He nods. We do.

"Why, what's up?" he asks.

I start with *house policy*. I tell him about *four weeks in advance*. He laughs and tells me I forgot about *şpagă*. Then he winks.

"Who's *Şpagă*?" I ask. Marius chuckles, raises his hand in front of my eyes and rubs his finger and thumb together: *money.*

"Oh," I reply, with a resigned chuckle. "What a surprise!"

He moves closer, speaking in a quiet voice.

"That's how it works", he confides. "I'm a regular. They look after me, I look after them."

Late-night traffic roars past the hotel. A white stretch limo peels off and drives towards the lobby. We split and go our separate ways. Marius turns, as if he wants to tell me something.

"I hear you went to Africa?" he asks.

"Yes," I answer. "Got back last night."

"How was it?" he asks apprehensively, "lots of black people?"

"140 million in Nigeria," I say, walking backwards. "Nice folks, in my experience."

"But is it true corruption is a big problem?" he asks, climbing into his car.

The Wrong Place

The elderly lady with the hennaed hair seems keen to chat, trotting after us on scuffed stilettos, tugging at her purple polyester skirt. She wears purple sunglasses with a diamanté motif. She's elegant in an old-fashioned way, but pushy too.

"Need a room, gentlemen?" she asks, poking her hair as she follows us down the rocky path with little old houses on each side.

"No, thanks," replies Horea, adjusting his knapsack, "but my English friend may buy a house. Do you know any?"

The lady stops and peers at me over plastic rims under a high morning sun. The mountain silence is broken by bird-song and a faraway train, chugging gently through fir trees that shoot for the sky.

"Yes, of course," she smiles. "Mine!"

Two minutes later, she's showing us round her home, a tiny cottage made from pastry and brown sugar. It nestles at the bottom of a triangular meadow, among slopes of potatoes. A large fluffy dog hops in a circle, barking. She hugs it fondly.

"I spent twenty euros on vet bills, even though I can't afford a banana!"

The dog wags its tail, as if it might have preferred the banana.

She shows us pokey rooms with haphazard carpets, a *soba* and a 3-D picture of a lake.

"I rent to hikers like you, very cheap, 50 lei per night," she says. Horea inspects the cramped bathroom and flashes me a sceptical look.

"Coffee, gentlemen?" she asks, leading us out like a tour guide.

We follow her down the slope into a tiny kitchen. On the wall hangs a framed photo of our host as a young beauty.

"I'm *Tanti Dorina*," she says with a friendly wink and tells me to sit on her bed. "And how do you like our little town of Tuşnad?"

I tell her it's very nice but we got lost in the forest.

"Five hours," explains Horea, "Because the *pension* gave us dodgy directions."

Tanti Dorina mutters darkly that we chose the wrong place:

"I know that pension. It's on Billionaires Row! Pots of money and none of it clean."

She shakes her candy-floss head and clucks like an old hen. Tanti Dorina has good skin, quick brown eyes and an easy laugh. Over tasty coffee, she chats non-stop about how she worked for a German business in Bucharest.

"They chose me because I'm Hungarian, not Romanian. There's a difference, you know." I press for details, but she is distracted by the arrival of her cat, who gazes at Horea as if to say *what's your game?* Tanti Dorina fusses over her pet and tells us it's good to have friends. But her graceful fingers betray inner anxiety. Soon we find out why. Her husband died twenty years ago. She has one son, but *sees the white crow* more often. He ran off with his daughter's friend, because his wife slept around. Then he lost his job and struggles to survive.

"Now I have nobody," sighs Tanti Dorina. "Even the cat is too busy these days with kittens." Then she starts to cry. She seems lost in her own home. She dries her eyes and tells me I can have it for €54,000. Horea chokes on his coffee.

"I bought it when I retired," continues Tanti Dorina. "But I made a mistake. It's in the wrong place. I forgot I would grow old. I forgot about that hill, it's too hard. I walk up it three times every day, collecting hikers from the station. They rent my room for 50 lei per night."

Personally, I'm not so sure. Tanti Dorina's bed is damp. I feel as if I am sitting on a pile of wet carpets. I want to advise her to air it, out in the sun. But that would be rudc. Instead we swap phone numbers and I give her a bar of Swiss chocolate laced with whisky. As we leave, I notice the number on her front door: *54*. I mention the coincidence."It's negotiable," she replies.

Horea and I head back up the steep rocky path. En route, we greet Tanti Dorina's nosey neighbours, who watch us in silence with narrow eyes.

We stroll through the town. Horea shows me the hotel where he stayed twenty seven years ago, as a child.

"Has Tuşnad changed?" I ask. Horea chuckles and replies:

"What do you think?"

We buy cheap *vafe* ice-creams and sit on a bench. Knots of school-kids amble past in summer clothes, giggling. Wobbly pensioners carry plates of food onto a battered terrace. Outside a swish looking café, a big gang of young adults in corporate T-shirts sit around a guy wearing a bush-hat and bandana, who explains about team-building. Some of the team are listening.

I tell Horea that Tuşnad seems to be suffering from an identity crisis. Half of it seems to be on its knees, locked in a subsidized past. The other half seems keen to reinvent itself as a modern, up-market spa with Internet and cable TV. "Let's hope the investment pays off," I add.

"Are you going to invest in that house?" asks Horea, as if he doesn't know the answer.

"Poor Tanti Dorina," I sigh, "caught between the past and the future, on a damp bed."

In the evening, we walk back to Billionaires' Row. Teenagers scurry towards our modern *pension* lugging big plastic bottles of beer. At midnight, I can hear them yelling and jumping on the floor above my head. Down the corridor, a guy screams at football on TV. Then at 3 am, the tanned blonde in the next room starts gasping and moaning in ecstasy, for a good ten minutes.

Oddly enough, none of this was mentioned in the brochure. We chose the wrong place.

Labyrinth

It's a good movie, according to the magazine. I look closer. The ad says the film is showing at Cinema Z, fifty minutes from now. I'm tempted, because *Pan's Labyrinth* was released several months ago and this might be my last chance to see it on a big screen. So I hurry uptown, a forty-minute walk on a humid day, under a blistering sun. By the time I arrive, my goose is cooked. I feel like a medieval pilgrim at the gates of Jerusalem. I enter through ancient doors, with sweat trickling down my back, shoes dusty, my throat parched. Just in time.

The lobby is empty except for a middle-aged couple playing backgammon at a table. Tiny white dice pirouette across an old wooden board marked with red and black chevrons. *Clack-clack!* The pieces are slapped into place by an expert hand. Eyes spin towards me. The guy is about sixty, unshaven, a chin of salt-and-pepper stubble. His shirt hangs open to reveal a wrinkly white vest. His opponent is a curvaceous woman in her mid-fifties, with long dark hair, a faded blue cotton dress and flip-flops that have seen better beaches. They look at me, then at each other, then at their board game. She sips coffee. He puffs on a cigarette and spits tobacco.

"*Pan's Labyrinth*?" I ask, hopefully.

The guy stands up, walks towards me. I assume he's going to open the tiny ticket office and sell me a seat. Instead he moves outside onto the steps, powerful forearms thrust deep into his baggy pockets. He sucks on his cigarette then tosses it into the gutter. He looks down the quiet street and shakes his head ruefully, as if the world is a strange place. He walks back inside and sits down at the backgammon board. He casts the dice then slaps his pieces down, *clack-clack!* He plays fast, seems to know exactly what he's doing.

"No film today," he murmurs.

I wait for an explanation, but none follows. So I check my little magazine, just to be sure. Yes, I'm in the right place, on the right day, at the right time. I show him the page, pointing at the tiny advert for Cinema Z.

"Excuse me, but isn't there a screening at one o'clock?"

The guy frowns at me. The woman folds her arms tightly, frowning at the backgammon board, looking for ways to whip his ass. Then she speaks for the first time since I arrived.

"Only if we get four clients," she murmurs, without looking up. She's determined to win.

"Pardon?" I reply.

"Maybe some more people will come?" adds the guy.

I get the impression he hopes not. I glance at my watch: three minutes to show-time. Pigs will fly.

"But what if they don't?" I ask. He shrugs again. *Not my problem.* His tired eyes turn towards the lobby, as if suspicious. I track his gaze. Behind me, a tiny kid is checking the poster. He wears a tatty pink Adidas T-shirt and a curious expression. I want to yank him in. But he vanishes. No *Spiderman* today. I turn back.

"Why do you need four people?" I ask.

"Because electricity is expensive," replies the dark-haired woman. "We can't justify it."

"But what about your advert?" I ask, brandishing the little magazine like a Bible seller. "How do you justify that?" She cranes her neck over the low ledge that separates us.

"Advert?"

"Yes, madam. The one that says you'll show *Pan's Labyrinth* at one o'clock, today. It doesn't say *but only if four people turn up because electricity costs too much.*"

Neither of them bats an eyelid. He cradles his stubbly chin in a hairy hand. She holds one of the backgammon pieces in mid-air over the old board, as if unsure of her next move.

"They're the rules," she mutters. *Clack-clack!* He scratches his head, staring at the board like he didn't expect things to go this way. He's not the only one.

"May I see your boss?" I ask.

"He's in Timişoara," says the guy, scooping up the dice like a Vegas pro.

"I don't believe this," I moan. "It took me over half an hour to walk here."

"Sorry about that."

"*Sorry*? You can't just advertise a film and then not show it. What kind of a place is this?"

"This is Romania."

Ah, I almost forgot. But then I remember. I move towards their table.

"No, this is Europe."

They swap glances like they've heard of that place. It was on TV at New Year, with fireworks.

"Your turn, Stela," says the guy. I watch them, puzzled. I almost envy them their indifference, because it protects them, keeps them safe. They know what's important – taking it easy with cups of coffee, cigarettes and backgammon. Living by the rules and not getting stressed, certainly not about some film, even if your job is to show it. Stela spins the dice and clacks her pieces.

"I knew you'd do that," says her wily opponent, chuckling into his chest.

"How much is four tickets?" I ask. Stela glances at me with wide eyes, black and shiny like olives.

"Forty lei," she replies, as if daring me to buy them. But I give up, on principle and on account of my pocket. I start to laugh.

"You know, I'm a journalist, and this is going to make a good story."

They exchange another glance. Their heads swivel towards me, like a pair of owls. I shrug in despair and slink to the exit, a beaten dog. I'm halfway there, when the penny drops.

"*Domnul!* Mister!" says Stela, scurrying towards the ticket booth in her flip-flops, brass key in hand. Evidently, the price of electricity just fell.

Five minutes later I'm sitting in the small empty cinema, all alone. The lights dim. The air is cool and makes a welcome change from the hot day outside. Two meters above my head a small square casts a pale glow of white light into the blackness. I watch a thousand specks of silver dust, dancing in the dark. The stubbly guy pops his head through the hole and whispers:

"It's only a DVD, will that be OK?"

"That will be fine, thank you," I reply.

Then I watch the film. It's in Spanish with Romanian subtitles, but I can cope, because the story is easy to follow. It's about a cruel world where nothing makes sense, and a little kid who takes refuge in fantasy.

Faith, Hope and Chablis

Petru is in a panic and trying to hide it. I can tell from his voice down the phone. It's slower than usual, like he's in trouble and carefully assessing the best way out. He mentions the baptism of his young son, Claudiu, aged eleven months. Seems it has taken a long time to organize, bringing scattered families together. Now they're in Bucharest. But he needs help.

"No problem, Pete," I say. Because I know he likes the English version of his name. I know it will remind him of the depth of our friendship. We don't see each other often, but we're solid. Or are we? The line goes silent and I start to wonder. I get the feeling he's wondering too.

"It's family stuff," he says, eventually.

"I know what you mean, Pete," I reply. "We all have families."

"Not like mine, you don't."

I listen while he explains. His French in-laws have just arrived in Romania for the big event: the baptism of their first grandchild. But they don't like their hotel. They don't like the food, they don't like the weather, and if Bucharest is Little Paris, *je suis Mickey Mouse.*

"They sound like a pain in the *derrière*," I suggest. "Do you want me to take them back to the airport, is that it?"

"No, I want you to make them happy."

"Who, me?"

"Yes, because you speak French, and lived there three years, didn't you?"

I stand on my balcony, watching *le trafic* with wide *yeux*.

As agreed, I collect Marie-Paule and Philippe from the lobby of their hotel. She has immaculate hair, a silk scarf and fine shoes. He sports a dark blazer with gold buttons and dandruff on the collar. They are both charming and extremely well-educated. I can tell from the way they talk about epochs and architecture. I begin to think Petru may have exaggerated the extent of his dilemma.

"The opera, what a marvellous idea!" chimes Marie-Paule as our taxi speeds alongside the river. She has cool gold spectacles, bright lipstick and a girlish giggle to her voice – not bad for sixty plus.

"In fact, *Cosi* is one of our favorites," announces Philippe. His eyebrows are large and bushy, the sort where potatoes grow. He insists that I call him *Piot*, because all his friends do.

They are delighted with our seats in the box. They know all the words and they sing along in low voices. People turn to see who's making all the noise. I bury my head in the programme. Piot starts conducting the orchestra with his right hand, swishing the air like he's killing flies. Onstage, a woman is *blestemată*. That means *cursed*, I know because I looked it up after my last opera. But hardly any men are *blestemat* in operas, probably because they were too busy writing them. In the interval, I take my new friends on a tour of the little museum upstairs. They like it, and I like them.

"Pardon?" says Petru.

I'm standing in my kitchen, stirring pasta so it doesn't stick, holding my phone in the other hand.

"They're amazing," I reply. "So clever, they know all sorts, and very witty. Are you sure I didn't pick up the wrong people?"

Petru says he's very grateful and please-will-I-do-it-again-tomorrow. He's clever too.

In the National History Museum, Marie-Paule and Piot are spellbound. The ancient gold jewellery in the subterranean vault glitters on purple velvet. I've been here before, so I feel a bit of an expert. I stand beside them and offer my advice.

"It's Roman," I say, in a quiet voice.

"Actually, that particular piece is Dacian," replies Piot, walking away. Marie-Paule whispers in my ear:

"He's an archaeologist."

For the next hour, I tail Piot like a school kid, hanging on his every word. Marie-Paule sighs and gasps at the helmets, necklaces, rings and daggers. They swap opinions in loud voices and we soon have a posse of Romanians following us, like an official tour. A guard sits in a chair watching with suspicious eyes.

Later, outside, Piot blinks in the sun and chats to his daughter on his mobile.

"Sylvie, *c'était superbe!*"

Marie-Paule flashes me a foxy grin. *Oh-la-la!*

In the National Museum of Art, they gawk at the old icons and luxuriant Venetian kaftans, but glide nonchalantly through the modern Romanian masters as if we are shopping for wallpaper. I'm curious, to say the least. As we exit across the elegant courtyard, I ask why. Piot strolls like a royal dignitary on tour, both hands behind his back.

"Not bad," he sighs "but too derivative of our Impressionists."

I'm stung by this blithe dismissal of *The Spy* by Nicolae Grigorescu, of Ştefan Luchian's haunting self-portraits, Camil Ressu's epic *Harvesters at Rest*, Ştefan Popescu's *Street in Morocco* and Corneliu Baba's *Chess Player*, not to mention Tonitza, Stoenescu, Bunescu and all the rest.

"The only original artist," I reply, trying not to sound too peeved, "was the caveman who mixed rock dust with spit. Even Picasso made his name ripping off the Congolese, as you know. But that's hardly the point."

An awkward silence ensues. Piot knits his bushy eyebrows.

"Quite right!" he says, finally. *Romania 1, France 1.*

Next, we walk across to Ceauşescu's famous balcony and the monument to the heroes of the '89 Revolution. Piot photographs the balcony but stares in bemused silence at the monument.

"They deserve better," sighs Marie-Paule.

As we leave, an American in wrinkly shorts arrives at the monument to the heroes, looks up and says in a loud voice *Jeez, it looks like shit-on-a-stick.*

In the tiny ancient church, it's time for the baptism. Little Caudiu gurgles and grins at the three priests in golden robes. A small choir sings sweetly under shafts of silver sunlight, their voices rise and swirl around the painted cupola above our heads. Guests mill about in smart suits and well-cut dresses. Petru tells me the old priest got the date wrong, and disaster was narrowly averted. His pretty Parisian wife Sylvie grips my hand; she cannot thank me enough for taking care of her parents.

"No trouble," I reply.

"Really?" she asks, looking rather unconvinced.

The three priests read from big books, chanting the prayers in sad voices that echo down the centuries, and around the church. Piot is scrutinizing the frescoes with an expert eye. Marie-Paule is beaming at her grandson. Incense billows around the baptismal font as Claudiu is undressed and brought forward for his big dip. He laughs and chatters as the priest lowers him into the water, kicking both feet to make big splashes, clearly delighted to be a Christian. When they lift him out, he howls and wriggles.

"He loves to swim," whispers Petru, the proud father.

I sense that the power of ritual is wearing down my atheistic doubt like salty waves on a stubborn rock. I am suddenly filled with an intense sensation, a yearning for some lost love. I realize I miss the past, those countless hours I spent dressed in red and white, fingers steepled to heaven, a good little Catholic. I remember being an altar boy, swinging the incense, ringing the bell, pouring the wine. Did I really want to be a priest? I think so. Something about helping poor kids in Africa.

The choir is reaching a climax. The priests are waving their arms and walking in a circle, Claudiu is giggling and people are wiping tears from their eyes, including me. It can be a cruel and nasty world out there, but in here we share faith, hope and paper tissues.

I move towards the door, to gets some air. I smell smoke, but not the sweet sort. Through a chink I spot yellow flames. There is a fire in the antechamber for devotional candles.

I nudge the door open. A scared-looking teenager turns and stares at me, helpless. He is wagging a newspaper at the flames, trying to put them out. But of course they shoot higher, licking up the old wall. He tips water into the smoldering tray of melted wax. It spits and roars and more flames shoot out. It's clear that if we don't stop it soon, the whole church could go up.

"Not like that," I tell him, "We need a rag and some water!"

We rummage around and find a piece of torn linen, about a meter square. It's perfect, possibly divine intervention. We douse it in water and stretch it above the flaming candle rack. We count to three and let it fall. The fire spits and hisses in defiance. The flames diminish and the little room fills with acrid smoke. We add more water until we are sure, then we retreat into the corridor outside. The frightened-looking lad tells me it wasn't his fault. I believe him.

The guests leave the church, smiling and chatting.

"Something is burning!" announces a lady with sequined lapels and a large pink hat. I tug the door of the antechamber and smile.

When the church is empty, the teenager speaks rapidly to the old priest, who seems oddly amused by the tale. He shakes my hand and tells me *Pope John Paul II slept in the big house across the road.* I try to look impressed. He takes a call on his mobile and turns away.

The reception is held in a posh suite in a nearby hotel. The Romanian guests cluster in one corner of the room while the French delegation gathers in another, fifteen yards away. This is not because of animosity, but cultural physics. They are propelled by a centrifugal force – their common language, culture and family connections. Nevertheless, it looks like *us-and-them.*

I help to ferry snacks and goodwill between the two camps. Sylvie uncorks expensive champagne, Petru distributes it in fine glass flutes. The bubbles soon begin to work their magic. The two groups fray at the edges and gradually meet in the centre of the room.

"They're lovely people," explains Sylvie, with a discreet nod towards her French parents. "But they can be very condescending to Romania and Petru's family. It drives me to distraction."

"Your folks seem OK to me," I reply, trying to reassure her. "Certainly very clever!"

Sylvie rolls her eyes.

"Too clever at times!"

"How do you mean?"

Sylvie guides me to a quiet corner, for the gory details.

"Within a few hours of landing, my parents had even managed to annoy not just all the Romanian guests, but most of our other French guests too! It seems my uncle told my dad *if you don't zip your mouth, Sylvie will disown you!* And you know what, Mike? He was right."

Then she's off again to distribute bottles of chilled, specially-imported Chablis. Piot wanders up, smiling proudly.

"My daughter knows her grapes, I made sure of it!" he tells me.

By the end of the afternoon, he's quaffing Romanian red – *Sec de Murfatlar* – and enthusing loudly about its *peppercorn attack* and *raspberry finish.*

Elderly Romanian gentlemen gather around to watch him, nodding in agreement. They have bright eyes and quick smiles. A small bottle of fruit brandy appears on the table: *palincă* – Romania's secret weapon of mass inebriation. The crystal liquid shimmers with medicinal promise. Piot agrees to try some. From nearby, Petru gives me a mischievous wink.

When the reception ends, we step from the hotel into the last rays of sunshine. The air has an April bite to it, but summer is coming and anything seems possible. Everyone is smiling and saying goodbye. Petru gives me a hug. Sylvie whispers her thanks. Marie-Paule clutches my arm, invites me to their cottage in the Loire. Little Claudiu wanders about, mumbling nonsense at the daisies, followed by Piot who bends over his tiny grandson to offer wobbly words of encouragement: "Yes, yes, Claudiu! But in French?"

Buried

43° C, the hottest day of the year so far. I decide to walk up town, just to see how it feels. No point hiding indoors, better to adapt, that's how humans survive. Plus, there's something I need to do – find out about Romanian writers. The Internet helps, but not much, Wikipedia offers only sketchy profiles. I want to read Creangă in his own words, see what the wilful ruralist was up to. Caragiale too, seems he has a barbed wit. Maybe even Iorga, the historian who was shot by fascists.

I make my way through tight streets, keeping to the shade. Not many people out today, the city centre seems quieter than usual. I walk past the fruit and vegetable market at Piaţa Amzei. I remember shopping here in my first week in Bucharest, in 1994. I bought a big bag of juicy oranges from Portugal, or so I thought. Now I know better: *portocală* means orange.

I find the library in an elegant old villa. Suspended over the entrance is an ornate domed canopy of glass and wrought iron. It looks like a giant clam-shell. The wide lobby has several smaller rooms leading off. Three women sit behind a counter, chatting quietly as they sort through books and tickets and papers. They seem surprised that I should want to register. They seem concerned when I mention Romanian authors.

"We don't have many of their books in English," the lady in the polka-dot dress tells me. But she's friendly and efficient and I am soon filling in an application form.

"What do you do?" she asks.

"I wear several hats, but mostly I'm a writer," I reply.

"I see, and where do you work?"

"These days, I work at home, mostly."

She gives me a funny look.

"No, I mean where is your desk?"

Now it's my turn to give her a funny look.

"By the window," I reply. I have a feeling one of us is missing the point, probably me. Maybe she means *what business do you work for?* But that's my business. All I want is a ticket to borrow books.

She stares at me for a moment, then sighs and ticks the box marked *intellectual.* She has shiny red nails, and holds the pen with her thumb and three fingers. I used to write that way, until a teacher said it was wrong. I wonder why. I wish he could see my box marked *intellectual.*

I walk down a short corridor into a medium-sized room with good natural light and some beautiful wooden bookcases. Old guys in suits and hats browse the shelves. The ladies were right: the English section is pretty small. I scan the shelves, left to right: Brontë, D.H. Lawrence, Dick Francis and a hundred others of varying credibility. But no Romanians, how come? "English translations are hard to find," explains a beautiful young librarian. She smiles sweetly from behind her heavy desk of polished oak. Her hair cascades in corkscrew curls onto bare brown shoulders, backlit by the morning sun. She appears to have a halo, like she's in an advertisement for shampoo. She's quite a picture. No wonder there are so many guys in here.

I return to the shelves, disappointed but determined to find something after my long walk in tropical heat. I flip through a dusty volume of Thoreau. A phrase jumps from the page: *a written word is the choicest of relics.* Perhaps that's why I can't find the ones I want.

Someone taps my arm, a delicate touch like a butterfly. I turn and find the young lady from the shampoo ad offering me a book. It's old and yellow with dog-eared corners and a familiar face printed on the front: Mihai Eminescu, the national Romantic poet with the rock-star looks.

"In English, buried in our cupboard!" says the librarian, with a perfect smile. I thank her and open the book.

The poems are lyrical, dreamy and evocative. I have a soft spot for Wordsworth and his *impulse from a vernal wood,* so the style feels familiar, reminds me of school exams. It's not quite what I was looking for, but something draws me in. For a translation, the language has an authentic fluidity, the metre rises and falls just at the right time, the rhymes are not forced. Eminescu had a good translator for this collection. I turn back the pages, keen to find out who.

A youthful face gazes out from the fly leaf. The young man looks about 18 years old. His features are symmetrical and very Romanian: strong nose, firm jaw and dark eyes – intense but mischievous. He looks like someone who would relish an argument as much as a joke. But like so many images from Romania's infamous 'Golden Era', this one has a slightly surreal quality. It is halfway between a painting and a photograph, as if the printer lacked proper equipment and had to falsify the final result. But if 'the medium is the message', this is a perfect visual reminder of an era when nothing was real: black was white, up was down, and if they really did paint the grass green for the president, why wouldn't they ink a photo? The young man's name is *Corneliu M. Popescu*. Below the picture is a copy of his signature flowing across the page. The characters are regularly spaced. He seems sure of *Corneliu,* which is written with a strong hand. But when he writes *Popescu*, the characters wobble as if he is not so sure about his place in the real world. I get the feeling he's a clever kid. But did he really translate all these beloved poems? There are dozens. I'm intrigued, now.

Overleaf, young Corneliu describes his approach to the challenge of translation. He seems to have an intuitive grasp of English, a poet's passion for nuance and an academic's curiosity for linguistics. He thanks his parents *who devote all their forces to preparing for me an active and useful life in society.* He makes special mention of his mother. An only child, you see.

His father, Mihai, adds a biographical note about his talented son. But the first paragraph makes my eyes pop: young Corneliu died in the 1977 Bucharest earthquake, aged 19. His translation of Eminescu was published posthumously. It explains his dad's adoring prose, but it doesn't explain the loss. What could? His father's notes ache with parental grief. After a few pages, I feel like someone sucked all the air from my lungs. Tragedy does that to you. I find a seat by the window and read on. The beautiful librarian gives me a smile.

Even allowing for a father's love and retrospective embellishments, Corneliu was a gifted individual. It seems his earliest teachers spotted it. He had extra classes and excelled at school.

By the age of 10, he was translating Robert Louis Stevenson. At high school Corneliu began translating Eminescu, hoping to finish the task before enrolling at medical college. He was also keen on maths – one of those rare students who can master arts and sciences. His dad was a lawyer with an avid interest in humanistic issues. From the age of 13, Corneliu attended conferences in Romania on science and world affairs, where he met Nobel prize-winners, diplomats and VIPs, chatting to them in English, learning, honing his language skills. He also made several trips abroad. A warning light flashes in my brain: weren't Romanians who travelled a lot during Communism usually 'connected', in some way? Maybe, but should that diminish the dedication of a talented boy?

There are some more photos – Corneliu with his parents on holiday in Transylvania, grinning at the camera. In another, Corneliu's hands are deep in his pockets and he smiles wide as he strides confidently forward, his winter coat unzipped on a sunny day. His mother follows a few paces behind, small and stocky, with the same distinctive eyebrows but a weary expression, as if life is not so easy with a prodigy. Again the photos have been retouched and have a spooky, almost supernatural quality to them, as if mother and son floated down from the sky.

The biographical note works towards its inevitable, shocking finale. Mihai Popescu describes how his wife and young Corneliu both died at home in the earthquake of March 4. There was a fire too. Reading between the lines, it seems their bodies were found entwined, as if seeking refuge in each other's arms, as if hoping to survive together or perhaps not to die alone.

Corneliu M. Popescu is immortal!, concludes his grieving father. A touch grandiose, but maybe Thoreau was right: words are our most important relics. I turn the page to find a simple but evocative line-drawing of a mother and son embracing. Opposite this is printed the first Eminescu poem as rendered by his teenage translator, a century or so after it was written.

And should it be together that we shall die one day
They shall not in some cemet'ry our separate bodies lay
But let them dig a grave near where the river flows
And in a single coffin them both together close
That I to time eternal my love beside me keep
For ever wail the water, and we forever sleep.

The little library suddenly feels too claustrophobic. Every other book seems irrelevant. This is the one I came for, I know it now. I walk out of the wood-panelled room and stand at the reception. The lady in the polka-dot dress asks me if I want Ion Creangă in French, they found it upstairs.

"No, thank you," I reply, "this will be all."

She stamps my card: three weeks' loan. Then I leave the library.

Outside, the sun is at its peak. The gods want to make horseshoes on my head. I stash the old yellow book in my bag and cross the road, towards the shade. My head is still spinning, but I can't help noticing an old building with a crumbling façade looming dark and high above me. It would surely tumble like a house of cards at the slightest tremor. I find myself wondering how it feels to perish in an earthquake. Is it a quick death? Or do you lie under tons of masonry, as the life is slowly squashed from your broken bones?

I think about young Corneliu, gasping his last breath. They say some men call for their mother as they die. But I doubt it brings any consolation, unless she hears you.

Author's note: In 1982, the *Corneliu M. Popescu Prize for European Poetry Translation* was established. Co-ordinated by the The Poetry Society (UK), it continues to attract many contestants every two years.

Free

It's time. Time to do something that I've been putting off for too long already. Something that requires forms and photocopies from all over town. I dig out my passport and a beige folder tied with string. Before long, I'm on the street below my block. I need a cab. Here it comes.

The taxi driver wears a neatly-pressed polo shirt of fine cotton with bright horizontal stripes. He looks like a stylish golfer. His after-shave smells of cinnamon. He's affable enough, until we drift into a nasty traffic jam. He spots one of his colleagues cruising past us in a capped-sleeve T-shirt, in the opposite direction. They beep horns and exchange a quick word but, beneath the bonhomie, something is not right. I'm not sure what. But my driver keeps turning around, checking his mirror and muttering under his breath. Finally he reaches for his walkie-talkie, clicks the button and chuckles down the line.

"Where's your T-shirt?" he asks. Static fills the ensuing pause, before the reply comes.

"What do you mean?"

"We're supposed to wear polo shirts or T-shirts, not vests. It's in the rules."

"What rules?"

My driver turns to me and rolls his eyes, as if to say *can you believe this guy?* He pulls the walkie-talkie closer to his mouth. He's not smiling anymore.

"In the green rule book, everyone gets a copy. Didn't you read it?"

We stop at traffic lights. At 40° C, the sun feels like a giant blowtorch welding us into our seats. Today, somewhere in this baking city, old folks will die. Same as last week, falling like pins. An angry voice barks down the radio at us. It's the other driver. His temperature is rising, too.

"I never saw any rule book! Are you some kind of smart ass?"

My driver listens, and gives me another exasperated look.

"No, I'm just saying we're not supposed to wear vests!" he replies. "We are supposed to wear polo shorts or T-shirts. Respect for the clients."

"When I get some clients," snaps the other guy, "I'll bear it mind. And by the way, where I come from, in Pantelimon, what I'm wearing is called a *T-shirt*. Got it?"

The walkie-talkie hisses and pops with static. My driver shunts his car through a gap.

"T-shirts have sleeves," he says. "Yours hasn't got any sleeves. There's a difference."

"You can say that again," scowls the voice down the line. "Where are you from?"

"What?"

Horns beep and scooters zip around us like mosquitoes. The other guy laughs through static.

"You sound like a hick. From Moldova, are you? Get out of my face."

"That's not very polite."

"Listen, I saw Mr. Sorin and Mrs. Lucia back at the office, and you know what they said? They said *Hello, Bogdan.* They didn't say *where's your T-shirt, Bogdan*? So if it's good enough for the boss and his wife, it should be good enough for you."

"I'm just trying to give you some friendly advice."

"Me too. It's a free world. Get lost."

The line clicks and he's gone, in search of peace, quiet and clients who don't mind sweaty biceps. My driver sucks his teeth and maintains a stoic silence until he drops me off at my destination.

After a forty-minute wait at the front desk, it's my turn with the middle-aged clerk. But after a four-minute chat, I know exactly what she is going to say. I can tell from how she's looking at me, the way she's shuffling my precious documents into a haphazard pile, her lips pursed like a conscientious cleaning lady. They're painted cherry red to match her ceramic earrings. She leans across the counter and passes the documents back to me. Here it comes.

"You need another stamp. To prove your papers are in order. The office is across town."

I close my eyes, in despair. When I open them, she's scribbling an address for me. I thank her, grateful for small mercies. Someone pushes past me and peppers her with questions, someone who ate garlic last night, possibly a truckload. I leave the musty building with its long, amorphous queues of fed-up Romanians, all watching that front desk with hopeless eyes. They're better-dressed than fifteen years ago, but little else seems to have changed. I tuck my documents safely in my knapsack, then walk down the worn marble steps and out onto the roaring street. I check my watch. I need another stamp. But first I need another cab.

The second driver drops me across town. We exchange maybe three words en route. He doesn't seem keen to chat with me or anyone else. He ignores his walkie-talkie, which barks requests like a jilted robot. I pay him and climb out. At the kerb, I find a family of Roma – gypsies, if you prefer – lined up in front of me: mum, baby and four kids, all dressed in clean clothes with dark fluffy hair, the older ones lugging bags stuffed with groceries.

"Is that cab free?" asks the mum.

"I guess so," I reply, holding the door open for her. She leans in and asks the driver:

"Are you free, *Domnul*?" He takes one look at her and shakes his head. The Roma woman backs off, looking puzzled. I know how she feels. Not because I've ever been the victim of ethnic prejudice, but because I still think my driver was free. Except perhaps from ideology. Or maybe he's had too many run-ins with *those people*, and they blur into one – *they're all the same.*

I tail the Roma family across the road, heading the same way as them. The boys wear smart shoes with polished heels. The girls wear pale pink sandals that match their dresses. They're all spotless, hair washed and wispy in a light breeze. The baby wears a clean bib and gazes back at me, balanced precariously on the hip of a pretty girl who is eight or nine years old. Mum spots another cab. She walks up and leans in. As I pass, I slow down, curious. This taxi driver is reading the sports pages of a newspaper.

"Are you free?" she asks. Without looking up, the driver nods, folds his newspaper and reaches for his meter. But his hand freezes in mid-air when he sees his new client. He shakes his head, unfolds his paper again and slides down into his seat to read. The Roma woman backs off, and says something to her little gaggle of kids. They groan in disappointment, eyes screwed tight. She scans the street for another cab. Her dark eyes meet mine. She shrugs. This is as close as we'll ever get. I walk off, threading through knots of dark-eyed Romanians, all scurrying towards democracy.

Right and Wrong

It's him again. Domnul Vlaicu, the Administrator of our block. I recognize the insistent knocking at the door of my apartment: six or seven sharp raps, like he's the police and I'm a bad man. I leave my desk, walk into the hall and peep through the spy-hole. Vlaicu is standing in the corridor dressed in baggy shorts and a white vest, with armholes that gape to his bony ribs. It's not a pretty sight.

I open the door six inches and look through the gap. He places his hand on the other side and pushes, as if he has right of entry. I block the door with my foot. He looks puzzled.

"Hello, Mr. Vlaicu, how can I help?" I ask.

"By letting me in," he responds, staring down at his clipboard, flicking crinkly pages.

We sit at my kitchen table. Vlaicu glances around my home as if checking that everything is to his satisfaction. He seems pleased with himself, patting his silvery quiff as if he's expecting coffee any minute. But instead I glance at my watch, hoping he'll get the message. Eventually, he rotates his clipboard so it faces me. Then he nudges it towards my side of the table. I scan the top page. It looks like some sort of petition, and presumably I am expected to sign it.

"Remember I said we need a lightning conductor on the roof?" asks Vlaicu. I nod, sitting back and folding my arms, intrigued.

"Well, I think I've found a solution!" he adds. His bright blue eyes shine with joy. "You see, *domnul* Michael, I've been approached by a corporation specializing in modern telecommunications. They want to put a radio transmission aerial on our roof, plus a lightning conductor to protect it. And best of all, they will pay us two hundred dollars a month if we let them! So, I'm collecting signatures and if you wouldn't mind… it's the right thing to do!"

He offers me a blue ballpoint pen. It's always blue ink, here in Romania. Because if you sign anything in black ink, they can say it's a forgery or a photocopy. Whoever *they* might be.

"You mean a mobile phone company?" I ask. Vlaicu smiles gleefully, raising his bushy eyebrows. They resemble two grey ferrets that just woke up and are having a stretch. He jerks the pen at me, as if puzzled that I'm not rushing to share in the financial bonanza. I try to look deeply concerned. He sits back, frowning at me now. "Is something wrong, *domnul* Michael?"

I tap my fingers on the table, wondering how to say it. He's sure to get angry.

"You know there might be health risk from all those radio waves?" I reply.

I'm not even sure I believe it, but I've learned that a little resistance keeps our esteemed Administrator on his toes and prevents delusions of grandeur. Vlaicu rolls his eyes and waves a hand, dismissively, like he's swotting summer flies.

"So what? We could get killed by a car tomorrow. At least this way we'll make some money. It will reduce everyone's bills. Surely you won't deny us, especially on our tiny pensions?"

His blue eyes glass over, as if he's about to weep. When I reach for the pen, he grins.

A week later, we meet by chance in the lift. Administrator Vlaicu nods as if trying to remember who I am. He clutches his old briefcase, no doubt full of forms about bills and parking.

"So when's the aerial coming?" I ask. He shoots me a glance. He seems to have no idea what I'm talking about. I try again. "Did you get everyone's signature, for the installation?"

Finally, he twigs.

"Oh, that?" he replies, vaguely. "No, our neighbour on the top floor refused to sign. So we lost the contract. The company offered it to the residents of the next block instead. Typical!"

He gazes down at his scuffed brown brogues, apparently dejected by this turn of events. For a moment, I feel a twinge of sympathy. He's a bureaucratic bossy boots, but life cannot be easy on a pitiful pension, especially with no kids to look after you.

"The guy on the top floor, why did he refuse?" I ask.

Vlaicu sighs and gives me a suspicious look, as if I know very well.

"Because he's made a little garden up there and likes to sunbathe, he doesn't want an aeriel spoiling the view. Also, he worked in radio communications for thirty years and he says he knows how dangerous it would be."

As we rise through the floors of our block, I watch the red numbers glowing in the wall of the elevator, like fever. Maybe the guy upstairs is right? But something doesn't add up.

"Thirty years? If it was so dangerous, why didn't he get a new job?" I ask.

Vlaicu shrugs, evidently past caring. The lift stops, the steel doors slide back with a squeak and he steps out. But I have one last question, so I keep the doors open with my toe.

"*Domnul* Vlaicu, if a transmitter is dangerous and if the phone company builds it on the next block twenty meters away, surely there's still a risk, especially to our neighbour upstairs?"

The Administrator scratches his head and gazes down the gloomy corridor full of mutant rubber plants. I get the distinct impression that he would rather be talking to them, than to me.

"That's exactly what I said," he replies, deflated. "But the fool wouldn't sign."

A police siren wails in the distance. Dogs bark far below in the car park. Night is falling, winter is coming. Our bills will be rising soon enough. Two hundred dollars would've helped.

"Oh well, that's life!" I suggest.

Vaicu glances around as if worried about spies. He moves closer, speaking in a low voice.

"*Domnul* Michael, I'll tell you something. Our block has been here over thirty years, but we've never had a lightning conductor and we've never been struck. Not even once!"

I can't help wondering why this fact has not occurred to our Administrator before now.

"So maybe we don't need a conductor, after all?" I suggest. Vlaicu nods in agreement.

"That's exactly what I said!" he snaps, with an impish grin. But now I'm confused.

"You mean, to our neighbour upstairs?" I ask, lost.

"No, that's what I told the Administrator of the next block," replies Vlaicu, flicking the leaf of a rubber plant.

Dust falls to the tiles in a tiny grey cloud. He looks at me with clear blue eyes, like a Victorian hypnotist. His skin is translucent, not a blemish. He's over seventy. He reminds me of a waxwork. I'm lost for words. He leans closer, keen to explain.

"I told the Administrator next door that it's simply not right that they should make money while we all get sick. It's not fair. I mean, after all, who needs a lightning conductor?"

Norwegian Wouldn't

I tell my taxi driver the name of the cinema, but he hasn't got a clue.

"Never heard of it," he replies, shrugging his shoulders up to his hairy little ears. A pink Virgin Mary dangles from his mirror, like she wants to help. We're sitting at the traffic lights. They're on red. I pull out my little notepad and flip through the pages of inky scrawl.

"OK, maybe I can help," I say. "I got this address from the Internet. Please, look."

The driver glances at my notepad, wrinkling his nose as he reads.

"OK, let's try," he replies. Then he starts revving his engine, like he means business.

"But maybe you should use the walkie-talkie?" I suggest, "Just to be sure?"

"HQ?" he says, with a sceptical look. The car suddenly jerks forward. The green light flashes past my head. Soon we're in fast traffic. He tells me my Romanian is not bad. I tell him learning the grammar is like trying to grab soap in the bath.

"Do you speak English?" I ask.

"Norwegian," he replies.

My eyes pop. Come again? Turns out he met a stunning Scandinavian girl in Bucharest. They got married, went to live in Oslo and had a son.

"I picked up the language in six months, just like that." He snaps his fingers for effect. I sit in the swerving car, wondering. *Doesn't Norwegian have unusual letters and tones?* It's not like he learned French or Spanish. He must be a genius.

"So how was Norway?" I ask, "High standard of living?"

He nods three times. But his smile seems tinged with regret. His lips tighten as he scans the busy city. Then he sighs.

"You wouldn't believe it, *domnul*. So civilized, so clean, modern, everything works!"

Except marriage, it seems, because now he's divorced. And his beautiful Norwegian wouldn't eat tripe soup.

"So where's your son?" I ask. He looks at me as if to say *what a dumb question.*

"Bucharest, of course. If he was in Oslo, he'd never come back. Think about that."

I watch kamikaze cars with black windows, thinking about it. At least the lad will speak Romanian.

After twenty minutes bobbing and weaving through the traffic, we arrive in the neighbourhood where my cinema should be. Except it isn't, nor is the street that I jotted in my notepad from the map on the Internet. Instead, there's just a maze of crusty apartment blocks and two teenage girls in hot pants sitting in a stairwell. One chews her hair, the other chews gum. My driver is watching them.

"Try the walkie-talkie?" I suggest.

"What?" he asks, as if he'd prefer to stick around. I tap my watch.

"Please, we have to hurry."

He shrugs and drives to a kiosk, where a gang of beefy middle-aged guys are sucking sunflower seeds. My driver asks for my notepad. I hand it over. He summons a stocky guy in a vest who is leaning against a knobbly grey tree, spattered with fresh dog pee. He has a bulbous nose and jet black hair like a wire brush. He is sipping coffee from a plastic cup. It looks like a thimble in his fist. He walks up to the taxi and squints at my pad like it's a crossword puzzle.

"Huh?"

"The cinema, where is it?" asks my driver. The guy pulls at his tracksuit crotch and says:

"Nothing like that round here, try the town centre." Then he looks closer at my notepad, pokes a stubby finger and says: "By the way, you spelled the street wrong. You missed an 'm'."

His mates around the kiosk laugh at the dopey Westerner.

"Thank you, *domnul*," I reply.

"With pleasure," he says, and pops a sunflower seed into his mouth. We trundle down the street, avoiding pot-holes. It's like driving over a giant waffle. Never mind a 4WD car – around here you need 4WD shoes. The place is like a war zone, minus CNN.

"So?" asks my driver.

"I copied it down right," I reply. "I checked three times! That website gave me the wrong address…"

I twist in my seat, peering at the dust cloud behind us, puzzled. My driver knows better.

"There's nothing like that around here. Plus, you spelled it wrong. You forgot the 'm'."

"Oh, really?" I reply. He smiles and shrugs, like it's pretty obvious to anyone with a brain, such as himself. I try to imagine him a few years ago, in a gleaming Nordic flat with under-floor heating and a communal sauna down the block, explaining to his tearful blonde wife why their son could not possibly be brought up in Oslo. I wonder how you say *goodbye* in Norwegian.

"Shall we go uptown?" he asks, swinging the car out of the boondocks and into a busy junction. I check my watch again.

"No, thanks, it's too late, just drop me at home."

"But the cinema is uptown. I thought you wanted to go?" he replies.

"I did, but you didn't know how to find it, remember?"

He looks disappointed. This could have been a lucrative fare.

"Sorry about that," he murmurs, "What was the film, by the way?"

"*Blood Diamond*, with Leonardo di Caprio."

"Is it any good?" he asks. I scratch my head, wondering how to answer.

"I don't know," I reply, "I haven't seen it yet."

"Oh," he says. He drops me off and says *sorry* again. He's a nice guy, I suppose. I give him a tip. But not the one I'd like to. I'd like to tell him to get a new job, teaching Norwegian.

Peace

"Want to come to a funeral?" asks my friend Lumi, as we rummage through our grey steel mailboxes in the lobby of our block, extracting junk mail. At first, I think she's joking. But no, she's serious and sad. She's been crying, buckets of tears. She has wet red eyes, like a carp.

"Who died?" I ask quietly, staring into my box. Someone's nicked my *Economist*.

"Uncle Gheorghe. He had Parkinson's, remember? You met him, six months ago."

I think back to our Brăila trip. *Six months?* It seems like six years – must be this long hot summer.

"Yes, OK, I remember, the guy with the difficult brother?" I reply. Lumi brightens up.

"Thanks," she says and walks to the lift. "It's on Monday. I don't want to go alone. There's trouble brewing about money. Train is at 7 am, from Bucharest. I'll buy your ticket."

The elevator doors close before I can say *actually, that's not what I meant.*

Next day, we buy flowers from the Roma ladies near our block. Their stall sits in an area that local estate agents might call *bohemian:* cobbled streets and rubbish up to your knees.

Still, Lumi says the ladies are helpful and not too expensive. So we sit and wait while they construct two wreathes – *coroane* – from flowers and fir branches, fuse-wire and bits of wood.

One of the ladies probably weighs about fifteen stone and wears a tight white disco outfit with a plunging neckline and high heels. She has a tough face and red lipstick. Her dyed blonde hair is bright yellow, tied back and flowing into a long ponytail. She chews pumpkin seeds and spits insults at a skinny fellow at the next flower stall, because his *manele* turbo-folk music is too loud. She's right, but he just grins back at her across the cobbles, as if to say *so what.*

Big shiny cars arrive, driven by guys in office clothes and mirrored sunglasses. They haggle over prices for huge bouquets. The Roma ladies haggle back in sing-song voices. A small van pulls up. The ladies heap flowers in the back and it drives off. As it passes us, Lumi points to the logo on the side of the van. It shows the name of an internet floral supplier and a website.

"The guy who owns that website charges three times more than I'll pay here," says Lumi, watching the van disappear around a corner.

"Because he's the middleman," I reply. "That's where the money is."

"And he has to grease palms all along the chain," sighs Lumi.

"I imagine funerals are quite a lucrative business?"

"You bet," Lumi replies. "Just wait until we get to Brăila. Remember Virgil?"

A cute brown puppy in a pink bow trots up to lick my knuckles, because that's where the salt is. *Virgil?* The name rings a bell. Then I remember: the difficult brother, dollars in his eyes.

On the train to Brăila, Lumi looks like a young nun. She's dressed all in black, with a black silk scarf in her hair. But she looks better than recently, as if she has come to terms with her favourite uncle's passing. Our two wreathes sit on the wire rack above us. Some of the other passengers make sad faces at us and we make sad faces back at them.

As the endless, flat farmland of Muntenia rolls by outside, I get the whole back-story. Uncle Gheorghe was born in 1925. Normal childhood, basic education, met Tanti Aneta and married young, no kids. Once a year he would stay in a monastery praying and helping the monks to do whatever monks do.

"He was a very devout Christian," says Lumi, "until he went to prison."

I turn away from the window and stare at her, across the gently-swaying carriage.

"Prison?"

"Seven years."

"Why, what did he do?" I ask, intrigued. Lumi tries to smile.

"Nothing, he was framed."

It seems a small amount of cash disappeared from the office where Uncle Gheorghe worked. Some wise-guys fingered him and he was too mild to refute the charge.

"In prison, they beat the life out of him," continues Lumi. "He came out a changed man – always sick with this or that. Tanti Aneta says that's why he got Parkinson's, but I doubt it."

"Were you close?" I ask.

Lumi nods emphatically and tells me about nicer times. Uncle Gheorghe used to take her for walks and once taught her how to lie on her tummy in the mud after a river flooded, to scoop out fish stranded in deep hoof-prints left by the local cows.

"I can still feel those little fish wriggling in my hand," she says, with a wistful smile.

Uncle Gheorghe also helped her with her reading. Tanti Aneta would make nice clothes for Lumi and her three sisters, who now live abroad and send little parcels now and then.

I listen entranced by these golden memories of an innocent rural childhood, from the days before Romania's milk-and-honey socialist fantasy curdled to an ill-nourished nightmare of long queues and vindictive spies.

"Uncle Gheorghe would not steal, he was a good man," says Lumi, tears in her eyes.

The cemetery lies on the southern edge of Brăila, near a beautiful big forest. The small chapel has painted walls and sits under a big old bell that looks like it should be on a Spanish galleon or in a Mexican village. Large, bare-chested men with spades and suntans walk around in mucky shorts with T-shirts over the heads, trying to keep cool under a boiling sun. Big cement trucks roar along a busy highway, to build something new. Romania is booming. The ground vibrates like it's time for an earthquake. A thousand skeletons must be dancing in their graves. It's as close as they'll get to the party.

Uncle Gheorghe is in the chapel, lying in a rough wooden box, with a tight grey face. He seems to have shrunken since I last saw him. His hair is neatly washed and combed, his suit is pressed and his little white panama hat rests alongside his head. His small hands are crossed on his hollow tummy. Little old ladies in black hunch on gnarled benches nearby, grim-faced. Lumi and I pay our respects then back out to wait for the service to begin. It's running late.

"The drugs gave him cancer of the liver and prostrate gland. He was in great pain," explains Lumi, as we take a narrow path through the graveyard. Identical headstones sit in tight rows like big boxes of cornflakes in a supermarket.

"Not much space in here," I remark. "Why is it so crowded, with all this land nearby?"

"It's private," says Lumi. "Big business these days, like you said. Every inch counts."

The sun is high in the sky and temperature must be hitting 35 degrees. It's almost unbearable, even for us. I think about Uncle Gheorghe. I try to imagine how it would feel, in this heat, to be cooped up in a tiny apartment that stinks of your own urine, with hands that shake even when you sleep and cancer nibbling your guts for ten years. Poor Uncle Gheorghe, what a way to go!

"He stopped eating, couldn't pee," continues Lumi. "The doctors told him to drink more water. He said it didn't help and that he wanted to die. They told him he would, soon enough."

We wander back to the chapel and sit on a low wall. Lumi briefs me on the various mourners as they arrive.

"See that lady getting out of the red Dacia? That's Tanti Maria, who lived near us when we were kids. And that man in blue? That's my dad's third cousin, daughter lives in Australia."

But when a tough-looking guy in filthy pants appears, with dusty sandals and a faded black shirt slashed open to a hairy chest, Lumi just stares. The guy looks familiar to me. I've seen him before somewhere. But I can't place the face.

"And who's he?" I ask. Lumi hisses air through her teeth, shaking her head.

"Oh, that's Gheorghe's brother, Virgil," she replies, under her breath. "He's an asshole."

Now I remember. Virgil struts about with a business-like air. He seems to have spent the morning digging his garden. He whispers to little old ladies, pats the priest on the arm, stands with his hands on his hips like he's running the show. For all I know, maybe he is. But I'm curious. Lumi provides the details as mourners slowly fill the little chapel under the big rusty bell.

"Last week, when Tanti Aneta knew Uncle Gheorghe was near the end, she called Virgil to ask for help preparing the funeral. Virgil agreed on condition that she sign their apartment over to him, to sell it. Tanti Aneta said no, because it's still her home. So he told her to get lost."

"Yes, of course," I reply, as her family jigsaw falls into place. "He wanted it months ago!"

I watch a long fat worm wriggling through the soil at my feet, as if it knows dinner is on the way. When I look up, Virgil is shaking hands with a trio of ladies dressed in black. He accepts their condolences graciously, with a pained expression and a hairy brown hand pressed flat to his heart. His pants are covered in grime. Lumi watches, kicking her shiny black heels together.

"So when Uncle Gheorghe finally died, Tanti Aneta and a woman from next door spent six hours washing the body and getting it dressed. You've seen how tiny she is? Seems a corpse weighs a lot and is very difficult to move, *rigor mortis* and all that. It's not a job for a widow."

"Why didn't she call an undertaker?" I ask.

"Too expensive! She'll never change – frugal mindset. If we send her money, she stuffs it under her sofa."

"Did she call you?"

"I called her. But she just kept saying *everything is OK.* Tough as old boots!"

"And that Virgil fellow?"

"He didn't visit her even once, and wouldn't help or give her a lift. Tanti Aneta had to ask friends and neighbours to help organize the funeral, seems it's been rather difficult."

"But what about your mum and dad?" I ask. "Couldn't they help?"

Lumi groans in despair.

"They live out in the sticks. Plus, my dad's useless, he says funerals scare him. By the time my mum found out what was going on and came to Brăila to help, it was all sorted. Tanti Aneta is angry, especially with Virgil. He keeps nagging her about money."

Right on cue, a dusty Dacia enters the car park and out steps the grieving widow. Tanti Aneta looks like she's been to hell and back. Her face is pale and weary. Her eyes seem to be receding into her skull. She walks with tiny steps, slightly bent, probably recovering from her stroke. But she smiles when she sees us.

"How are you, Lumi?" she asks, reaching with a frail hand. They hug but don't kiss, because it's considered bad luck and Tanti Aneta has had enough of that.

During the service Tanti Aneta sobs quietly. She leans over the wooden coffin, opening and closing her mouth like a fish, as if in silent communication with her dead spouse. I try to imagine her years ago, sitting alone at home for seven years while the entire street gossiped about her Gheorghe, the nice man who got locked up for theft. *No smoke without fire, right?*

The priest chants prayers and brother Virgil stands beside the coffin with big wet eyes, blessing himself three times every ten seconds, gazing on his brother's shrivelled body as if their parting will bring unbearable sorrow. Without a contract for the apartment, it probably will.

Then he takes a small wicker basket containing a small bottle of *ţuică* and a ceramic bowl of what looks like brown porridge. He begins moving the basket slowly back and forth over Gheorghe's little grey head. The priest and two choristers sing sweetly and everyone reaches for the sleeve of the person in front and starts pulling, gently, an Orthodox tradition pledging eternal memory of the dead.

The procession to the grave is undignified chaos. Tiny ladies in black jostle for position, until even Tanti Aneta is relegated to the role of a minor observer. The sky rings with the sound of pitiful wailing, but not from Tanti Aneta. She walks alone, her head down in tearful silence.

Lumi and I carry the wreathes we brought from Bucharest – the only flowers Uncle Gheorghe has received – but somehow we end up in the middle of the throng, instead of at the front. It's not our fault, because we did not expect this stampede of little old ladies. But even so, they keep poking us in the back with sharp little knuckles, muttering *get to the front, where you should be*. Hopefully, Gheorghe will see us trying.

We watch from the edge of the crowd as the priest leads the final prayers. A big tanned guy is stripped to the waist, pulling thick grey ropes and yelling instructions to his gravedigger mates as the coffin is lowered into the narrow hole. He has huge biceps, one of which is covered with a lurid tattoo of a bright green palm tree, like he's advertising bargain holidays. Tanti Aneta's name is already engraved on the headstone, under Gheorghe's. I ask Lumi how come, seeing that she is still alive.

"Tanti Aneta likes to plan ahead," Lumi murmurs, "Like a lot of people."

Tanti Aneta gazes at the headstone, as if checking that they've spelled her name right.

For the funeral reception, we retire to a large annexe uptown, with dark wooden crucifixes and painted icons hanging on white walls. It belongs to the church but smells more like a hospital – antisceptic and bleach, cabbage and roast chicken.

On the way to the big dining room, I pass the kitchen. The door is slightly open and I spot our large priest inside. His hand is in a big black cooking pot, scooping out food. He eats it and licks his fingers. He sees me watching and turns away. His broad back is covered in a black gown that drapes elegantly to the tiled floor.

Lumi and I join the other guests. There's about forty of us. I can't help but wonder: if Gheorghe has all these friends, how come his tiny widow got so little help when he died? Then again, most of them are probably wondering who I am and why I am here. It's a good question.

We are shepherded to the top table, which is set with plates of meat and cheese, bottles of water, baskets of bread and – best of all – little china bowls of sticky brown porridge, the sort I saw in Uncle Gheorghe's wicker basket. It's made from wheat, nuts and cinnamon. It's sweet and addictive, as I soon discover.

"*Coliva*," explains Lumi, popping an olive into her mouth. "Romanians eat it at funerals."

"Could you get me the recipe?" I reply, digging with my fork.

"Why, thinking of having a funeral?" she asks.

"One day," I reply. After a few minutes, Tanti Aneta joins us and huddles in a private conversation with Lumi and her mum. Virgil the brother-in-law watches them with unblinking eyes from his own table, chewing hard on a chicken leg. He's sizing me up too. I look away.

Later we take a rattling tram to Tanti Aneta's tiny apartment. It smells of pee. The polished wooden cabinets are stuffed with little porcelain dogs and books about Jesus and Lenin. On the walls hang brightly coloured photos printed from a computer and laminated with clear shiny plastic. Lumi takes one down for me to see: it shows two of her sisters in New York. They look like a couple of movie stars, grinning and strolling through a wintry Queens, with bright eyes and shopping bags.

"It's not real fur," she explains, pointing at their huge collars dappled with snowflakes.

Tanti Aneta sits on the wide sofa with her little feet hanging over the edge like a kid. She looks about seven years old, not seventy. Two little ladies in black fuss and fetch coffee. Lumi's mum sits back, dispensing tabloid wisdom on health. Lumi asks her to stop yapping, because she has something more important to say. The little sitting-room falls silent.

"Tanti Aneta," continues Lumi, "We want you to visit New York."

"Who's we?" inquires Tanti Aneta, clearly unimpressed.

"Me and my sisters, we'll pay the flight. You can have a holiday, take your mind off things while we get this place cleaned up for you, renovated."

Tanti Aneta knits her brows and pulls her lower lip between finger and thumb, thinking.

"But she's never been on an aeroplane," says Lumi's mum, who evidently has. She folds her arms like a seat belt and looks around the room through her big specs, as if that settles it.

"So what?" scowls Tanti Aneta, and gives Lumi a big wink. "Tell them I'm coming."

The two little old ladies in black stare at each other and then at their friend Tanti Aneta, as if she's lost her mind. She smiles mischievously at them, as if she's found peace.

Happy Holidays

It takes me a while to realize what's going on. Running does that to you, the mind drifts to quiet places as the endorphins kick in, and you end up in a sort of trance, where the only sounds that register are passing cars, because they can kill, and birdsong, because it is hypnotic. But today I am stirred from my dream-world by the activities of a group of young people down the road.

There are four of them – three beefy teenage girls wearing vests, short skirts and training shoes, and a little barefoot boy in baggy yellow shorts. They are all dark-skinned and sit on the long low wall facing the Parliament, dangling their heels in the shade and watching six lanes of speeding traffic. Four Roma kids enjoying the long hot summer in booming Bucharest. Or maybe not – they're probably bored, impoverished and have little better to do. I feel a bit sorry for them. Behind the kids a patch of rough land slopes back towards a dense clump of trees. Beyond the trees lies the rough part of our neighbourhood, where the local Roma live in dilapidated villas and where bad-tempered dogs sniff through piles of rubbish. Not much investment up there.

I'm running alongside the low green fence around the Parliament when I notice the girls scurry across the road,

200 meters ahead of me, dodging traffic. They hop over the fence on this side and approach a woman who is walking by herself. I run on, watching my step in case of pot-holes or dog pooh. It's a scorching day and I've got another hour of circuits to go.

Next time I look up, I see the four kids scurrying back across the road, but much faster. They seem to be in a big hurry. The woman they were talking to is standing with her hands on her hips, watching them. As I run past, I notice she's quite old and looks a bit upset. Her watery mouth is open wide – she just saw something bad. She raises two bony fingers to her forehead, looking puzzled. The skin on her hand is almost translucent in the bright light. Blue veins thread through milky flesh like thin rivers on a map. I follow her gaze to the four kids. They are scampering across the wide patch of rough ground towards the neighbourhood where the Roma live. One of them is carrying a handbag, but tosses it in the air. They disappear through the dark trees. I look back at the lady. She marches to a security gate a few yards away and taps on the dusty black glass. As I turn the corner, I finally understand what has happened. They robbed her.

The kids are back a few days later. I'm out running again, about 100 meters away, but with a clear view. The sun is high and the pavement stretches before me, empty of people. This time, the girls stay on their own side of the road, dangling their heels on the low wall under the trees. The barefoot boy trots alone through the traffic and sits on the green fence on my side of the road, as if waiting for someone. Sure enough, a young lad ambles around the corner, chatting on a mobile phone. He's about twelve. The Roma boy walks alongside for a bit, with his hand out as if begging pennies. The other lad waves him away and keeps walking. The Roma boy reaches out, grabs the phone and runs. The victim stands and stares, then pursues the little robber, yelling as he runs across the busy road. But the Roma kid is much faster. In seconds he's into the trees, where the girls are waiting. They vanish in a blur of colour. *See you, sucker.*

Third time, I'm jogging along the knobbly pavement at 5 pm. Not my favourite period, because it's rush hour and the air is thick with exhaust fumes, not to mention insults from loud-mouthed wise-guys in cheap little cars with big aerofoils glued to the back. I pull my cotton baseball cap down and nudge my shades up. Who cares – in ten minutes, I'll be cruising.

I see it all from 150 meters away. I know exactly what's coming and break into a sprint to intervene. I watch the three Roma girls ambling across the road, tailed by the little barefoot boy. There is a sense of purpose to their movements, not too fast, not too slow, like lionesses stalking their prey on *Animal Planet.* It's not personal. It's business, survival even.

The gang makes a beeline for three adults walking by the Parliament, one of whom is taking pictures. The Roma boy approaches, as if begging. The three girls fan out to surround the unsuspecting strangers. There is a brief scuffle. I hear a distant yelp of protest, carried on the summer breeze. Then the Roma kids turn and run back across the road, through the traffic, heading for the shady sanctuary of the trees. It's over in thirty seconds, *thank you very much.* One of the beefy girls is running so fast that her right breast pops from her baggy vest and bounces up and down, all creamy white. But she makes no attempt to cover herself. A passing driver beeps his horn. *Hey sexy.*

I arrive at the scene, panting and sweating from my 150 meter dash. Two of the victims – a middle-aged lady and a lad of about fifteen – are yelling at each other in German. The woman has tired eyes, no make-up, grey hair in a pony tail. She wears a hippy necklace of turquoise beads and a faded *Jack Daniels* T-shirt. The lad wears ragged jeans and expensive-looking shades. A large Nikon hangs from his neck with a zoom lens the size of a Coke can. He tracks the robbers through the viewfinder and clicks twice. Smart thinking, might help.

Standing with the two Germans is a slim woman in a smart linen suit, handbag clasped to her arm. She is yapping on her mobile in Romanian – sounds to me like she's calling the cops.

"What did they take?" I ask, looking towards the trees. The thieves are distant dots.

"My phone!" wails the German hippy woman, her arms spread wide.

"But I got some photos," says the lad, brandishing his big fat Nikon.

"You're lucky you've still got your camera," I tell him. "Those kids mean business."

"We thought they were begging for money," adds the woman, tearful and pale-faced. The slim Romanian lady is still blabbering into her phone, striding in circles.

"Follow me," I suggest to the two Germans, and they do, like lambs. We walk downhill to the nearest security post. The guard at the Parliament gate is dressed in a dark blue uniform. He stands legs apart with both hands behind his back, military style. He gives me a nod. I nod back. We know each other from my circuits around the Parliament. But we've never spoken, until now.

"You got tired," he announces, like he's wanted to say this for months. I shake my head.

"They got robbed," I reply.

He tilts his blue cap to the back of his head and looks at the pale-faced Germans.

"Oh, not again," he sighs, and unclips his walkie-talkie.

"Good luck," I say to the tourists, and continue my run.

Latin Driver

Eventually I find the address I need. The office is squeaky clean with modern chairs of tubular steel and black leatherette. The décor has a nice summer feel to it – pale lemon, beige. Bright light sparkles from lines of tiny bulbs on invisible wires, like a jeweller's shop. Ambient music plays from Bose speakers, pinned discreetly to the wall. The clerk is young and helpful, dressed immaculately in a neat linen suit. She has a firm jaw, a golden tan and hazel eyes that shine with sympathy as she tells me everything I need to know.

"They sent you to the wrong place."

Next stop: the notary. My young taxi-driver seems determined to shatter the land speed record. He's twenty years old, tops. We careen around corners on two wheels of screaming rubber. He seems to regard other vehicles as obstacles and pedestrians as second-class citizens. The car jolts as it rights itself. I ask him to slow down. He tells me he has to hit his quota, for his boss. Presumably the boss didn't mention hitting walls, bridges, cars, dogs or people. I ask him again to slow down. This time, he starts laughing and tells me:

"Relax, not dangerous! I'm different from you. I'm Latin! Same in Italy, Spain, yes? We drive like them!"

He floors the gas and we plummet up a long hill outside the Ministry of Defence. It's like riding a rocket to Mars. Any minute now we'll vanish into a Black Hole, emerge in Renaissance Rome and get burned at the stake.

"Don't you think the laws of gravity apply in Bucharest?" I ask him.

"I don't like politics," he replies, deadpan. The kid is either witty or has a death-wish.

At the lights outside Hotel Marriott, he slows down to suck his 2-litre Coke and ogle the car park, where a creamy white Porsche is tucked alongside a dove-grey Aston Martin. There's a also a yellow Lamborghini and a red Ferrari. He bows his head over stone-washed jeans and closes his eyes. Maybe he's tired. Or maybe he's praying, with a vision of himself pulling babes in a black 612 Scaglietti. But when the lights change to red, he's back with me in his yellow Dacia, ramming the gears like his bossy Latin mum asked him to mix a cake with a wooden spoon.

"So, did you ever drive in Italy?" I ask.

He shakes his head, swapping lanes at the last possible minute.

"Not yet," he mutters, with an optimistic smile.

"How about Spain or France?" I ask. My guts are heaving as if we are at sea.

"No," he replies, bombing around a bend. Then he gives me a suspicious look. "Did you?"

By now, I've had enough. I feel like I'm going to be sick. I don't see why it has to be this way. I decide to try shock therapy.

"Yes, I've driven in Latin countries," I reply. "And in my experience, most Latins don't drive like you. They do drive fast sometimes. But mostly they drive safely, in Europe at least."

Now he's laughing at me.

"Hey man, I'm a taxi driver, this is Romania! This isn't fast! You should see me when I..."

"But there is a place," I say, interrupting, "where lots of people do drive like you."

He glances at me, hooked, as if he's watching Discovery Channel with a six-pack and snacks.

"Where?" he asks, grinning, as he shaves the back of a bus.

"Africa," I reply.

My driver's head turns like an owl. He gives me a hard look. The grin evaporates. He slows down.

"Africa?" he asks, incredulous.

I try to guess what he's thinking. He's probably thinking *Africa-where-the-darkies-live*? But to be honest, right now, I couldn't care less what he's thinking. I'm just grateful we are no longer trying to break the sound barrier. He looks confused or in shock, he probably can't decide whether I'm trying to insult him.

A low-slung Hyundai Coupé slinks past us. It's a cool-looking machine driven by a willowy blonde girl who is puffing on a slim-line cigarette. But my driver doesn't bat an eyelid. He keeps glancing at me then back at the road, then at me again. Like maybe he's picked up ET.

So I tell him that many Africans seem to have a fatalistic attitude towards life, and that despite its many charms the continent has some of the most dangerous highways you could ever encounter. Highways where drivers drink beer and peel bananas at 90 miles an hour in big overloaded trucks that wobble at 45° and force you off the road, coming the other way. Move or die.

"Bananas?" he asks.

"They certainly are," I reply. "But the faster they drive, the more cash they earn. A bit like you I guess, except it's *not in their blood*, as you say."

He weighs it up, driving more slowly now, ignoring the honking traffic.

"OK, you can drop me here," I announce. He pulls over and gives me a receipt. I give him the money and a small tip. He pockets the cash and asks:

"Where did you go, in Africa?"

"Here and there," I reply. "But if you ever get the chance, drive from Kigali to Nairobi, or Abuja to Kano. They drive fast, so you'd probably enjoy it. Oh, and look out for the buses on fire in ditches, the mashed trucks and the dead kids hanging in trees."

He pulls the door and drives away, elbows hugging the wheel.

Miss Lawyer

The senior stylist in the local salon has immaculate hair – silvery grey blonde, cut short and neat. She wears a smart white blouse with the collar turned up and buttons undone to show her tanned cleavage. Her tight black Capri pants and dark blue ballet pumps combine elegance with practicality. She looks very glamorous and smells like a flower shop. She's about forty years old and very sure of herself, but I get the impression she's not so sure about me. I stand on the other side of the curvy white reception desk, looking down at her big diary as she runs a painted red fingernail through a list of names and appointments.

"Is it for you?" she asks, glancing up at my tufted skull. I nod, helpfully. Then she spots my name. "Ah, yes," she says, like a headmistress, "but could you wait five minutes? We're busy, as you see. Would you like coffee?" I agree and sink into a deep sofa, feeling like Penelope Cruz.

The salon is painted bright white, but some sections are peach-coloured, in contrast. A designer probably thought of that, very clever. The huge mirrors are spotlessly clean. The mosaic tiled floor glitters like a posh hotel on the Italian Riviera. Black beaded drapes line the windows and shiny steel racks line the wall, full of lotions and potions. I try to remember how hair salons used to look in Romania years ago. Times have certainly changed.

All the ladies who work here have blonde hair. The two clients in the black leather seats have blonde hair. The air smells strongly of ammonia, presumably because the rest of Bucharest wants blonde hair too. I browse the glossy photo-magazines, where beautiful people wear black suits, chat in cafés, poke at their cool white Apple Mac laptops, or lounge on yachts. They're mostly blonde too. Even Secret Agent 007 is blonde these days. *Maybe I should dye my hair?* Then again, I don't have any. Maybe that's why the stylist was puzzled. Because after months of do-it-yourself with an electric shaver, my head just looks sort of... patchy. Like a convict. Or so my friends say. Anyway, who cares, I'm paying. I sip hot coffee and wait, skimming the pages.

The front door jerks open and a familiar face peeps through the gap. It's the woman from my block – second floor –, the one who pretends to be friendly but is actually rather difficult; the one who refuses to co-operate with any ideas, especially good ones; the one whose mother is a full-time nutcase and throws her black cat off the balcony, if it says the wrong thing. The one they call *Domnişoara Avocat*, Miss Lawyer. They say she's a brain-box. She's certainly a bit of a busybody. I lower my eyes to read an article about broccoli, this month's Miracle Food.

"I want you to do my hair," announces Miss Lawyer, marching in. She twists at the hips to show the stylists a long matted pony tail that hangs from her head like oily rope on a merchant ship. Her hair appears to have been bleached several years ago, but now it's mostly grey. It's a bit of a mess and looks like it needs some styling, preferably by a sheep shearer. Her faded black dress sits on her like a tent. She wears red shoes with Cuban heels and scuffed toes. She looks like she could be an extra in the opera, for *Carmen* maybe. As usual, there is something odd about her manner, as if she likes to provoke people so she can then accuse them of being unreasonable. Me versus The World – perhaps she learned it from her batty mum.

The glamorous senior stylist seems to sense trouble. She stops snipping her client, puts a firm hand on her shapely hip and watches from the mirror.

"Oh, really?" she replies, in an uncompromising tone. She exchanges a sideways look with her blonde colleague who is hunched over a white porcelain bowl, kneading mousse into a client's head. I have a feeling that both of the stylists have met my neighbour before.

Miss Lawyer glances around the salon. Her skin is pale grey and her tired eyes are lined with heavy mascara. She looks like a panda. I sink lower behind my magazine, trying to hide.

"I haven't got much time," she barks, at anyone who will listen. "So where do I sit?"

"I'm afraid you need an appointment," sighs the senior stylist, finally turning from the mirror. The second stylist watches, raising a fine eyebrow behind her pale green designer specs.

"Why?" snaps Miss Lawyer. "It will only take ten minutes, just a trim!"

"I doubt it. You'll need a proper appointment. We are very busy, you can't just. . ."

But Miss Lawyer interrupts, waving her hand, as she has no time for nonsense.

"I'm too busy. I never know when I'll be free. I want you to do it now. Shall I sit here?"

She points to an empty chair in front of the mirrors. The senior stylist twists her shiny red lips into a steely smile, and points around the salon with her scissors.

"Sorry, we have two other clients to finish. And then there's this gentleman..."

Silence falls. Under the bottom edge of my magazine, I see red shoes approaching the sofa. Miss Lawyer peers around my page with inquiring eyes, like a turtle checking a beach.

"*Domnul* Michael," she whispers, "what are you doing in a ladies' salon?"

She smells of fried onions.

"I need a haircut," I reply, looking up. She stares at me as if to say *you need your head examined.* She scrutinizes my scalp, presumably checking for lice.

"Does he have an appointment?" she asks, still scanning my head with her X-ray gaze.

"Yes," says the senior stylist. "And by the way, for your hair, I think we'll have to charge at least 100 lei. It needs a good cut and some proper attention."

My neighbour spins on her heels, squaring up as if she plans to punch the stylist in the nose. The other clients watch from the mirror. One has a head covered in white mousse, like an ice cream cornet.

"So?" snaps Miss Lawyer. "You think I can't afford 100 lei?"

Nobody speaks. Music chimes from little speakers high on the wall. The Beatles are singing *All You Need Is Love*. After a moment, the senior stylist shakes her head and replies:

"I don't want to take your money and do a rush job, that's all."

The junior stylist in the cool green specs turns from the porcelain bowl to add her own opinion:

"Because it would not be fair on you, would it? We'll need an hour so we can cut it nicely, use conditioners, oil, mousse, whatever we think is best. It takes time. That's why you need to book ahead."

Miss Lawyer's eyes pop.

"Mousse?!" she howls. "Who said anything about MOUSSE? You'll do what I say! I'll decide what you put on my hair and how you cut it! I'm the client, yes!?"

The junior stylist shrugs and turns back to her work. She's had enough. The senior stylist checks the diamanté hands of the big clock on the white wall. Time is money.

"We've had this discussion before, madam," she sighs. "I don't have any bad intentions, I am simply too busy. I'm sorry, but I have to work." She returns to her client, scissors raised.

My troublesome neighbour seems to have run out of arguments. She sits beside me on the sofa and mutters quietly:

"*Domnul* Michael, are there any other hair places round here?"

I nod and point outside, to a row of shops on the other side of the busy street. As usual, Bucharest's hare-brained drivers are racing up and down as if cars are a video game. Brakes screech in the distance. Miss Lawyer frowns at the prospect of dodging all that traffic.

"Oh, forget it," she sighs, "I'm too lazy!" Then she smiles at me, as if we're on a date. She seems to want to chat, so I close my magazine.

"How's your mum?" I ask. But Miss Lawyer just gives me a funny look, gets up and marches out of the salon without another word.

Before long, it's my turn in the chair. I sit down and stare at my reflection, wondering why salon mirrors always make me feel like a tramp. No wonder stylists dress up. As elegant fingers wrap a silky shawl around my shoulders, I try to explain about my tricky neighbour.

"That lady looks after her mother, maybe it's difficult for her to plan ahead," I suggest.

But the perfumed senior stylist seems unmoved by the possibility of mitigating circumstances. She glances at her chunky orange Swatch. She seems less composed, now.

"Well, that lady should learn," she replies, knotting the shawl loosely at my neck. "Because we don't live in communist times anymore. In those days it was different – you could just walk in off the street. We'd have a line of clients sitting waiting. We'd fix them up, put them under the dryer and let them gossip for an hour. But it's not like that now. We take our time, do a professional job. These days, if you can walk in without an appointment, it's probably not a good salon. So if she wants me to cut her hair, then fine, but she must book and not make unreasonable demands. Anyway, never mind. What can I do for you?"

The senior stylist stands back to examine the haphazard results of my home-hairdressing. She looks puzzled, probably because my skull is covered with a centimetre of patchy brown fuzz, like the potato someone forgot. I watch her in the mirror. She taps her sparkling white teeth with a shiny red fingernail, head tilted.

"I want to look like Victoria Beckham," I reply.

Mermaid

Sibiu is on steroids. It used to be a sleepy town in Transylvania, with one foot in the Middle Ages. Now it's a European City of Culture for a year, with an arts festival every other weekend, modern paving and designer fountains in the square.

"The mayor's ethnic German," explains my host, George, proudly pointing out new developments as we walk through the busy streets where tourists sip coffee on sunny terraces. "So some people say he's not a real Romanian. They're never happy, no matter what. But he helped to get things done, as you can see."

I tag along with my heavy rucksack, just off the train after a five-hour ride from Bucharest. I'm glad to stretch my legs. Plus, we're hiking this weekend, so this is good practice.

We buy vegetables from the open-air market, where even the garlic has muscles. We buy pungent goat's cheese from the dairy hall, where women in white hats plead with us to try more, pretty maids all in a row. Then we head back to George's home, via some bookshops.

He lives in a small, cosy house in the corner of a large cobbled courtyard. Skinny cats peer down at us from balconies festooned with crimson geraniums in ochre pots, Italian-style.

George's pretty young daughter Catrinel comes out to help us with the shopping. She has pale brown eyes and pigtails. Inside the house, she shows me her dollies and tells me their names. Then she shows me an album full of her paintings, explaining each one. She seems to have an eye for colour and composition, a real little artist. She's keen to show me around and we move back to the cobbled yard, walking and talking in the bright sun.

"Do you know what you want to be when you grow up?" I ask.

"Of course," she replies. I listen carefully as she discusses her prospects, tells me her plans. For a youngster, she has some very grown-up ideas. But it's hot, so we sit in the shade on the kitchen steps, which are worn smooth like big grey pebbles.

"Two hundred years old," explains Alina, George's wife, from the kitchen. She's busy stuffing sweaters and waterproofs into a rucksack for our big walk tomorrow. Catrinel disappears indoors to make me a painting of wolves and bears, *in case we meet some.*

The house has beautiful parquet flooring and ancient doors with huge iron hinges like a medieval torture chamber. George shows me around, explaining how, actually, once upon a time, the room was a dance studio, run by two spinsters who left Sibiu during the Second World War.

"Jewish, probably," he adds. Alina gives me a wink.

"George thought he was Jewish for a while," she says. "His father told me he had read too many books."

It's a fair point. Their home is like a library: solid shelves of dark wood extend from floor to ceiling, packed with novels, biographies, dictionaries. George thrusts a sequence of books at me: battered copies of Mircea Eliade, Ionescu, Beckett and finally a novel by Canadian singer-songwriter Leonard Cohen, in Romanian. "Superb translation," he murmurs, flicking through.

Then he pulls down an older book, closes his eyes and presses his nose to the musty pages, sniffing like a pig after truffles. "I love doing this," he sighs, passing me another. "Try the Iorga," he suggests, as if it's the new Chanel.

After dinner we watch a film I brought from Africa. Catrinel sits between us on the sofa, staring at the screen.

"Where are all the white people?" she asks, quietly. She's very attentive and asks smart questions in German and Romanian. But after half an hour of black people and subtitles, she's fast asleep.

"She's cute," I murmur.

"Trouble-on-legs, once upon a time," replies her George, stroking his daughter's head.

"How come?"

"When she was five," he continues, "we had some friends over for dinner. As usual, they all took their shoes off at the door and Catrinel offered to help. Everyone was very impressed."

"Until it was time for them to go home," adds Alina, trying not to laugh as she gets up and disappears into the kitchen.

"Why?" I inquire. George leans back on the sofa and groans.

"Catrinel had put every pair of shoes in the bathtub and turned the tap on," he replies.

His helpful daughter is sleeping soundly by my side, warm and snug. We laugh, but not loudly.

"Is she good at school?" I inquire, with one arm around Catrinel's tiny brown shoulder. George nods but seems to have something else on his mind. After a moment, he explains.

"We were worried she might not get in. It's the best school around, and very popular."

"Lots of clever kids?" I ask.

George gives me a sceptical look.

"Lots of clever parents lying about their addresses," he replies. "If you know the right people, you can get your kid in, no matter how thick or lazy they are. That's probably why the teachers keep complaining that they get too many Grade 5 kids at Grade 2 standard."

Alina pops her head through the kitchen door.

"We live yards from the school," she adds. "So by rights, Catrinel should have qualified for a place, automatically. Plus she's smart for her age, always reading."

"But guess what," sighs George. "She had to sit an exam for one of the last few places. She was lucky to get in."

"Yet now she's top of her class!" concludes Alina, bringing a tray of coffee and sweet biscuits. She serves us with a breezy smile.

"I'm not surprised," I reply, stirring my little china cup. "Your daughter's very bright. She told me she wants to be an architect. That's pretty cool for an eight year-old. How come?"

George smiles but doesn't answer. He looks towards his wife, as if she can handle it.

"When we renovated the house," explains Alina, "an architect helped with the plans. Catrinel liked his plans and drawings, and so he told her all about his job. She was very interested. For weeks, she was doing her own little designs. But I'm not sure she's serious. She's a kid."

"Sounded pretty serious to me," I reply. "You never know."

But George seems to know very well, and is unconvinced. He grins to himself, threading tanned fingers through his mane of curly hair, pulling it over his eyes like a bored teenager.

"Don't be too impressed with our clever little daughter," he says. "Last week she wanted to be a mermaid."

The Result

Time to watch some more football! I enter the five-star hotel near my block and make my way to the sports bar. It's big but fairly empty, except for a gang of tiny kids having a party at the other end. They wear paper hats and bounce around on an inflatable monster. Their joyful shrieks pierce the air. A few older kids – aged twelve or so – stand around watching, as if trying to maintain their cool. A young woman in a hotel uniform is directing the fun, but the jumping tots don't seem to be paying much attention. They have their own rules. Or rather, they don't want any. They run and jump, push and pull. They squeal at each other and throw anything they can lay their hands on. A dozen bored-looking adults lounge at tables nearby, wearing casual clothes in bright colours, chatting among themselves. One woman wears large sunglasses. A young lad runs up to her table, howling his eyes out. She peers at him, over her gold frames.

Fifteen metres from the party, I take a stool at the bar. The TV is showing my team. But the sound is on mute. Two barmen are chatting as they stock the shelves. I ask the big guy for a juice *and the TV remote, please*. He pours my drink, but has bad news.

"Sorry sir, we have to keep the sound off."

"Why's that?" I ask, disappointed, because footy isn't footy without songs and chants, hiss and boo. The barman tilts his head sideways and says: "Because we're having a party, eh?"

He's about forty years old, with hairy arms and a body-builder's physique. His hair is cut short and he has a tiny hole in his left ear-lobe that suggests he once wore an earring. I track his gaze across the room, towards the gang of kids. They're whooping and yelling like little hooligans, high on sugar. Television? They wouldn't notice if a bomb went off.

"Are you serious?" I ask. The barman hands me my juice and shrugs: *rules-is-rules.* I sit in bemused silence, staring at the TV. The score is 0-0. I feel as if I am watching it under-water.

A girl from the party trots up to the bar. Her hair is well-cut and dyed blonde, three or four different shades, like a model. It must have cost a packet. She is very good-looking and wears pink lipstick, with a touch of eye-shadow. Her black jeans have a diamanté motif and her heels give her an extra inch. She's about nine but looks seventeen. It's a bit creepy. She puts an elegant red leather boot on the brass foot-rail, hoists herself up and shouts in a shrill voice:

"Coke!"

No *please* or *thank you.* The big barman serves her and she trots off, sucking her bottle.

"Nice manners," I say. We watch her tiny bum wiggling like she's on a catwalk. A slim blonde woman extends a lov-ing arm as she passes. The girl shies away. *Not just now, mummy.*

"Same every time," sighs the barman, folding his big arms. "I blame their parents, eh?"

"You're probably right," I reply, turning away to watch the TV.

"They come here in their big *soofs*," says the barman, "flashing their money."

"Big *what*?"

"*Soof.* It's an American word. It means Jeep, Range Rover, Land Cruiser…"

Finally, I get it.

"You mean SUV?"

"Yeah, *soof.* That's what they drive, big ones. Rich but no brains, eh?"

By now, I have the impression he's spent quite a lot of time with Canadians, *eh.*

"How do you know they have no brains?" I ask.

The barman rests his elbows on polished wood.

"Because when they sign the bill", he murmurs, "half of them can't even write!"

"So what," I reply, "plenty of smart people write like spiders."

He doesn't answer. He looks at me as if to say *you know what I mean.* I twist in my stool, glancing discreetly at the well-heeled entourage around the kids' party.

"So where does their money come from?" I ask. He shrugs and reaches for a bar towel. "I don't know, and I don't want to know," he replies.

He doesn't sound envious of wealth or privilege, he just sounds bored with it, or perhaps with his job. Yet from my observations, he's quick and conscientious, and likes things to be done properly. I can tell from how he stocks the shelves, turning the bottles the right way round. His shirt is neatly pressed and tucked in, his shoes are shined. He looks like a professional. But professionals don't gossip. So I'm curious. We get chatting. His name is Iulian. He talks slowly, with an accent that seems to have travelled from New York to New Zealand, via Toronto. He's affable enough, chooses his words carefully. He tells me he likes sport. But he doesn't like the way Romania is heading. He's noticed it more and more, ever since he came back from sea.

"I did four years, eh? Royal Caledonian Cruises! I served on *Queen of the Ocean*, *Horizon Princess* and all those big liners. Just for the money, eh? But then my parents got cancer and diabetes, so I came home to raise my kids. My wife prefers it this way. Fair enough, I suppose."

"How old are your kids?" I ask. Iulian reaches for his wallet, flips it open and shows me a photo of two young boys in roller blades and pads, hugging a tree as if they're scared to let go.

"Missed them like hell while I was away," he says, sadly. "But now I miss the cash. You can't win in this game, eh?"

"At least you travelled," I add. But Iulian's reaction suggests there's more to it than that.

"If you meet a Romanian who says he's on the ships to see the world, he's lying. It's always the cash. You can make a small fortune. Think about it: half a dozen barmen in one bar alone, taking between 2 and 3 k a day, with 15 percent tip on every drink? It motivates you, eh?"

I'm still trying to do his sums in my head when he leans closer, speaking quietly.

"Now multiply that by twenty bars on one ship and you'll see what I mean, eh?" He rubs his thumb and finger together, then stands back, waiting. I give up. I hate numbers.

"So, did the money change you?" I ask, changing the subject as politely as I can.

Iulian gives me a puzzled look.

"It's the experience that changes you, not the money," he says.

"How?"

He plucks a Carlsberg bar towel and starts wiping down glasses, like we're in a gangster movie.

"In lots of ways! I changed my attitude towards work and towards people. I'm not racist anymore. I used to have big doubts about blacks."

"Why?"

"Because of TV. I saw them getting beaten by cops, so I figured they must be bad, eh? On the ships, I learned black guys are just like us! I shared a cabin with two of them for six months. They were clean and polite, funny and hardworking. We became friends!"

"The world is full of surprises," I reply, checking the silent TV. *Damn. It's 0-1.*

"Not everyone was like me, though," adds Iulian, troubled. "I knew two Romanian guys who resigned after two weeks simply because they didn't like having a black boss."

"Jesus," I say. But I'm talking about the football. I can't help it. *Where's our defence?*

"That's nothing," says Iulian. "There was a guy from Baia Mare, up north. He signed on for six months, but onboard ship he refused to speak Romanian, only English or Hungarian."

I look away from the TV. This tale sounds a bit more interesting.

"Why?"

"Good question," says Iulian, with a sly grin. "At first it was sort of funny, like a bet or something. But soon we realized he was serious. He would criticize Romania, saying it's *dirty* and *horrible* and he'd *never go back*. I told him to stop knocking our country, or someone would break his neck, probably me. But he wouldn't, so we stopped being friends. He got his reward in the end, though."

My barman buddy pauses to stack some shelves with tonic water. He works quickly, grabbing three bottles in each hand, fingers splayed like the feet of a lizard on a wall.

"What kind of reward?" I ask.

"An American family joined the cruise, very rich. He got the job of looking after them on the ninth floor, where it cost $ 9,000 per month to rent a suite. He was hoping for big tips. They got chatting and he told his usual story about how he *used to be from Romania* but now he *hates* the place, *blah blah.* At the end of their cruise, guess what? They didn't give him a tip. Instead, they wrote *poor service* on his report card. The family were ethnic Romanians who'd emigrated to New York many years ago and now felt insulted by his rude comments. Our boss went nuts, eh? Demoted that guy for six months: assistant waiter, the lowest of the low!"

We both laugh. Iulian's younger colleague walks over and says "Watch out, I heard that."

"No offence, Doru!" says Iulian, wrapping a beefy arm around his skinny mate.

Doru is about twenty, with dark hair, gelled on top. He wears a leather bracelet and funky black shoes with pointy toes.

"Would you like to work on cruise liners?" I ask. At first, young Doru seems to think I'm recruiting for an employment agency, tapping talent. But I quickly explain I'm just curious.

"I prefer to stay in Romania," he replies. "The pay is less, but my mates are here."

"You'd make new friends at sea," says Iulian. But young Doru seems unconvinced.

"Are you single?" I ask and Doru nods, ruffling his hair, as if it might help solve the problem. He looks like a cockerel minus a hen. Iulian nudges him. It's some kind of private joke.

"Why not try six months, make some cash and see the world?" I suggest. Doru wrinkles his nose and fiddles with his bracelet.

"Not my idea of fun."

"You'd be surprised how much your ideas will change," suggests Iulian. "Mine did."

Doru shrugs and wanders off with a handful of shiny cutlery to lay tables. Iulian watches him, until a slim guy in a dark suit comes to the bar for a white wine spritzer. He's got *Le Monde* tucked under his arm and carries a smart leather purse, like he's in Paris. Iulian serves him quickly, reaching for bottle and glass but still chatting to me. He could work blindfold, I bet.

"A lot of young guys sign up because they think it's a way to emigrate. How dumb is that. *I'm gonna jump ship as soon as we dock in Miami, live in America!* That's what they'd say. So I'd tell them: *not for long, you've got 29 days' grace on your visa, after that you're illegal. You want to spend the rest of your life living in the shadows?*"

Iulian twists a paper napkin origami-style into a cute bud and sprinkles salted peanuts into a steel dish for the guy in the dark suit, who retires to a corner table, sipping spritzer.

"And would they listen?" I ask. Iulian shakes his head, emphatically.

"Uh-uh. They'd say *you wanna spend the rest of your life on a boat?* They were kids, thought they were smarter than everyone else. One of them ended up in Iraq as a marine, on some amnesty programme. Clever, eh? He could have travelled the world, made a nice pot of cash, then come back to manage a bar. Now he's sitting in some desert, shitting his pants."

I glance at the TV. The score is 1-1. I haven't seen any of the goals, but at least I'm not sitting in the desert. I watch

Iulian at work, trying to imagine how many foreign lands must be stored away on his mental hard-drive: all those ports and coastlines, all that big blue ocean…

"What was your favourite place?" I ask.

"Venice," he replies.

"And what about people, any favourite nations?"

Again he answers immediately, like we're on a quiz show and he wants the bonus prize.

"Good and bad everywhere, but my best mate was Jose from Honduras. We hit it off big time, eh? We'd chat for ten minutes every day. He said when he first saw me he thought I wouldn't last two weeks, *because I looked like a tough guy who wanted to fight.* I told him *no way José. When I work, I work. When I party, I party.* You have to be serious, right?"

One of the party kids runs up to the bar, hoists himself up and squeaks:

"Give me a Sprite!" Pretty soon, there's a long line of thirsty youngsters heading our way, barking their orders in tired voices. Iulian serves them one by one, with a blank expression.

"Earlier, you said you don't like the way Romania is heading," I remind him. "What did you mean?"

He lines three Cokes on the bar and pops their caps, quick as a flash. He could win contests. When he's done, he flicks the caps into a bin, from his thumb. One, two, three, like a cartoon.

"You can't change people," he replies, with a shrug. "Live and let live, eh?"

For some reason, I find his answer disappointing. Maybe I want him to engage, to try harder.

"I agree," I explain, thinking it through. "But I'm talking about education. You're wiser than you were, right? So, if you were chatting to one of your friends tonight and they made a racist comment, would you speak up or not? Would you pass on a little of what you learned?"

He raises his eyebrows, makes a face. For the first time in our chat, he looks lost.

"Who, me?" he asks. "I haven't thought about it. I dunno, maybe I would? But most folks I meet are only interested in how much money I earned. They're not interested in people or places. If I talk about some city I visited, they think I'm showing off. In fact, now you mention it, that's one of the things that bothers me."

"Why?" I reply, and Iulian gives me a funny look.

"Because they expect me to talk about money, about how I'm going to make it big. But that's not my style. I'm basically the same. I'm not one of those Romanians who swap their name to *Brad* as soon as they leave home, then blame the Americans who didn't like *Bogdan*. The only place I changed," he concludes, tapping a finger against his temple, "is up here. If you get out there and work in the world, the world works on you. If you want to survive, you adapt, eh?"

"Like the guy who went to Iraq?"

"That's up to him."

One last kid is waiting at the bar. He pulls himself up and hisses:

"Pineapple juice!" He's about ten, in a Batman T-shirt and designer jeans, with a gold earring and blond highlights. Iulian serves on autopilot. The kid leaves. No *please*, no *thank you*. We watch him swagger back to daddy, who gives him an approving wink.

"Maybe that little boy should work on the ships one day," I suggest, "and see life from the other side of the bar?"

But Iulian looks unconvinced.

"He won't need to. His mum's *soof* is probably bigger than my flat. He lives in a different world, the other Romania, the one in the adverts."

I glance up at the TV. To my disappointment, my football match has finished. Motorcycles are whizzing across the screen. That's what happens with the sound on mute.

"I missed the end!"

"Sorry about that," says Iulian. Then Doru appears carrying a crate of beer, his long skinny arms as taut as steel wires on a suspension bridge. He looks up at the TV.

"What's the result?" he asks. But who knows. We'll just wait and see.

Keep Off the Grass

It takes the gang of labourers six weeks to erect the little green fence. They work in shifts, often until late at night. I run past a few times each week, training for my marathon. They usually stop and stare. They seem to think I am training for the nuthouse. The fence is made of painted steel and measures 50 centimetres high and about 700 meters long. It runs down the western edge of the Parliament in Bucharest – the second-biggest building in the world – and encloses an area of rough ground about 2 meters wide. In places, this ground contains grass, trees and bushes. Elsewhere, it contains only litter, dog pooh and jagged concrete. Still, the men are building a fence around it, with their spades and blow-torches and welding masks and slow cigarettes. As they work down the verge, they leave clumps of concrete behind them, drying in the sun. To be honest, the whole thing looks a bit of a mess. I find myself wondering why we need it. Presumably somebody somewhere wants the place to look neat and tidy. Maybe this will help.

Next time I go running, I spot a large dog lying on its side under some trees, on a grassy patch between the new green railings. At first, I think it's sleeping in the shade. But no, it's dead. A full-grown German Shepherd. There is no blood, no bashed head or twisted legs. So it probably wasn't hit by a car. Maybe it jumped the fence and had a heart attack in the heat? Looks like it's been here at least a day, because its tummy is bloated and the air is starting to smell all around. I keep going. Soon I pass a woman in a street cleaner's uniform, picking up litter. Farther up the road, guys in similar uniform are hopping on and off the back of a garbage lorry. I stop running.

"There's a dead dog back there," I explain to the woman, pointing. "Perhaps your colleagues could take it away in their truck?"

She squints at me in the sunlight and says, "Good idea."

But the dog is still there the next day, and so am I, pinching my nose as I run past on the uneven concrete pavement. I switch to a narrow strip of rough grass, partly to avoid the smell and partly to reduce stress on my knees. Ask any runner.

"Hey!" shouts a security guard, stepping from his gate house outside the Parliament.

I glance around. He means me. I slow down, dripping sweat, and peep over the top of my shades.

"Stay off the grass," he yells, as I approach. I can hardly believe my ears.

"Pardon?" I ask.

"Run on the concrete," he says, pointing to the pavement. He is clean-shaven and has bright eyes of pale blue. His boots are nice and shiny, and so is his stick for whacking people. It dangles from his belt next to his walkie-talkie, gun and various items I don't want to know about.

"Why?" I ask. He seems bemused, as if ordinary people shouldn't answer back.

"Because the grass is trying to grow," he says slowly, emphasising each word.

"Oh," I say, "so how come it's full of litter and junk and never gets watered?"

"What?"

"And how come there is a big dead dog on it, back there?"

I point my dripping finger up the path behind me.

"It's been there a while and it smells very bad."

The security guard looks puzzled.

"Dead dog?" he asks, tilting his head and shielding his eyes, gazing into the distance.

"It's not very good for Romania's image," I add, "this being the Parliament and all."

"What?"

"Can't you call someone and ask them to take it away?"

The guard considers my suggestion for a few moments.

"Who, me?" he asks.

I leave Bucharest and return a month later. On my first run, the stench of decaying flesh hits me from thirty yards. The dead dog is still there, stinking and shrinking into the grass, with its matted grey fur pulled tight across its bones. The long grey snout has shrivelled up, exposing sharp white fangs that snarl in silence. Someone has even cut the grass, nice and short around the poor mutt, whose furred ribs now resemble a birdcage with an oily rag on top. It will soon be a skeleton. I jog by, pinching my nose. The dog grins at me like a cornered wolf.

Half a dozen guys in baseball hats stop and stare at it. Some take pictures with big cameras. I hear them chatting as I pass – American, French, Italian. They look like tourists. I wonder how far their pictures will travel.

Further down, the same guard is on duty as I run past on the rough grass. But this time he doesn't yell. He just nods at me and we say *hello.* I don't bother to mention the dog.

Nearby, the workmen are carefully erecting the last few bits of green steel fence.

Sacrifice

Ovidiu opens the boot of his shiny little Dacia and my buddy George dumps our three big rucksacks inside, ready for the hills. Ovidiu is George's neighbour. He has bright eyes set deep in a lively face, tanned and unshaven. He wears a baggy vest exposing thick arms that probably once lifted weights, but not for a while. He has hairy knees, brown feet and dusty yellow flip-flops. His belly sags over faded Adidas shorts, *World Cup 2006.* After brief introductions, he cracks jokes about the England football team.

"Not like the old days, eh?" he asks. I can only agree, and laugh.

We climb aboard and are soon cruising through Sibiu's low-roofed suburbs, heading south-west towards distant green hills. Little by little I notice we are going faster and faster.

George rides shotgun, upfront. I'm sitting behind with his wife, Alina. She's wearing baggy corduroy pants and walking boots. Between us sits their young daughter Catrinel, wearing a pink polka dot T-shirt, faded jeans and cute little walking boots, just like mum's and dad's.

Ovidiu twists his head and chuckles at us.

"Nice day for a hike!"

Not to mention a car crash. By now he's hurtling around country corners on two wheels, swerving to avoid oncoming traffic. I tap Alina on the knee and whisper sideways:

"Can you ask Ovidiu to slow down?"

"I can try," Alina replies, and passes on my request. Ovidiu chuckles again and sizes me up in the rear-view mirror, shaking his head wistfully. He appears to believe that the laws of physics are a western plot to deny him freedom of movement.

"Don't worry," he sighs, "I've been driving forty years. I know our roads!"

I watch the forest rush past in a squiggly blur of green and brown dripped by Jackson Pollock. I begin to wonder what Ovidiu would say if we crash and one of us gets spattered across the road like a pizza. Actually, I think I know what he'll say: *the other guy was driving too fast.*

Alina spreads a map across Catrinel's knees and nudges her with an elbow.

"Want to show Mike where we are going?"

Catrinel giggles and points with a tiny tanned finger.

"Cindrel," she replies. Ovidiu twists around in his seat.

"You should take him to Făgăraş," he suggests, "do some real climbing!"

Alina makes a face. Clearly she doesn't agree, which is fine, because neither do I.

"Făgăraş?" says Catrinel, with a puzzled look.

"Maybe next time," replies George, "when Mike's got his walking legs."

"And ten year's of mountaineering experience," I add, just for good measure. *Făgăraş.* Even the word is enough to put the willies up me. Ropes and rock and hard hats? Not just yet.

Catrinel pokes her mum and speaks in a quiet voice. "Mummy, that's where Uncle…"

But dad interrupts, turning to face Catrinel from the front seat.

"Yes, it is," says George, quietly. "But let's not talk about it just now".

When we stop for a loo break, Catrinel trots after her mum into the trees. Ovidiu strolls about, puffing on a cigarette and laughing into his mobile phone. George and I stroll along the side of the road, munching peanuts and stretching our legs. High above, fluffy clouds drift across a bright blue sky. A stream gurgles somewhere in the woods. It's picture perfect, Romania at its most beautiful. George is naming the plants, squinting in the sun. He stops and leans against a tree.

"Don't you love the mountains?" he asks.

"Of course," I reply. "What happened in Făgăraş?"

He grunts. Maybe I should mind my own business.

"Did I ever introduce you to Aurel?" he replies, eventually. "*Uncle Aurel*, as Catrinel says?"

I shrug, clueless.

"Mountain rescue guy?" adds George, "mid-fifties, big beard? Good mate, good fun?"

I think about it for a few moments, but no, I don't recall any grinning Grizzly Addams. I shake my head. George looks puzzled, but shrugs it off.

"Whatever. Last summer, we were playing chess in Sibiu. He told me it had been a good year so far in Făgăraş, not a single dead tourist: *no sacrifice* to keep the mountains happy."

"Sacrifice?" I ask, bemused. "He sounds like some kind of pagan priest."

"Not really, just a volunteer with twenty years of experience."

George's voice trails off into silence.

"So what happened?" I ask.

"Well, winter came and as usual Aurel was on duty in Făgăraş. One day, he rescued an injured skier, some greenhorn from Bucharest who got into trouble off-piste and called the emergency number. Aurel found him and carried him to a refuge. Then the guy says *hey, where are my poles? They're expensive – you better find them.* So, Aurel and a colleague went out to search again, even though that's usually considered bad luck."

George looks up, scanning the wide valley around us. He seems reluctant to finish the story, but knows I'm waiting.

"Aurel never came back. He got hit by an avalanche. They found his body in April when the snow melted. He was holding the poles."

Someone is shouting. We look up. It's Ovidiu, jabbing at his watch like he's in a big hurry and life is too short for chatting.

"Move it, guys, let's hit the road!" he yells.

George and I walk back to the car in silence, taking our time.

Turtle

It has to be done. But I'm not looking forward to it. Bogdan assures me everything will be OK. He just needs someone to come along for the ride. Just in case.

"Plus, you like dogs, don't you?" he asks, as if daring me to refuse.

"I like all animals," I reply, hoping it's true. Then we spend five minutes coaxing big brown Tess into the back of his car, with tasty titbits. At first, the Boxer is suspicious, but eventually the goodies get the better of her.

"She's never been inside," explains Bogdan, finally slamming the door. We climb in and drive off. Tess sits in the back, slobbering as if to say *got any more?* "Good girl," says Bogdan.

The vet's clinic is a thirty-minute drive across miles of flat farmland. When we arrive, Bogdan produces a well-made dog muzzle, made of tough fabric, the sort used for rucksacks.

"Imported from Germany," he says, slipping it over Tess' nose and tugging the straps. Then he fits a leash to her leather collar. By the time we drag her into the vet's operating room Tess is rigid with fear and seems to sense that bad things happen to good dogs.

The vet appears, unshaven and dressed like a butcher. He has a terse manner. He's more important than the rest of us. He doesn't smile or offer comforting words to Tess. He just pulls rubber gloves on, flicks a syringe and mutters: "Two hours." A solid assistant dressed in green cotton pyjamas hoists Tess onto the battered steel table. The dog looks terrified.

On our way out, I notice a small glass tank on a ledge full of plastic plants. The tank is the size of a shoebox, and half full of dirty water. Inside it, a turtle sucks for air. The container is so small that the turtle can't even turn round. Bogdan and I peep inside. I'm puzzled.

"Why would a vet keep an animal in such cruel conditions?" I murmur.

"No idea," replies Bogdan. "It's been here as long as I remember, six months at least."

He knows a café nearby and buys me a coffee. We don't feel like eating, somehow. I can't stop thinking about the turtle, locked in a glass cell. He can't stop thinking about his Boxer.

"My Tess is a slut," he says, one eye on a TV. "But after this, she can shag every dog in the village."

When we go back to the clinic, Tess is out cold. Her tummy has a horrendous slash up the middle, about 7 inches long, with big ugly stitches. I remember dog operations back home. This is far worse. She is bleeding like a pig at Christmas. Bogdan looks concerned.

The vet says *done* and turns away. Bogdan pays and we haul Tess onto an old sack, out to the car. She is as limp as a rag. Bogdan strokes her head and says: "Shit, I forgot the muzzle."

"I'll fetch it," I say, and trot back to the surgery. The vet drops the muzzle into my hand. It doesn't look right. Both straps have been severed.

"What happened?" I ask. He gives me a funny look – *who the hell are you?*

"Dog chewed the straps," he replies. I take a closer look. The straps have not been chewed. Anybody can see that. They've been snipped cleanly, with scissors or a sharp knife.

"Oh, really?" I ask, "Before or after the anaesthesia?"

The vet looks at me harder this time, and says: "When it was waking up."

But I know he's lying. Because right now, doped to the eyeballs, Tess could not chew fresh air, never mind two straps of tough fabric, ten minutes ago.

"I don't believe you," I reply. "Someone cut it. It was a good one too, from Germany."

The vet gnaws at his lip for a second and scratches his head, like he's a tough cop from New York, and I'm some crack-dealing punk.

"Son," he replies, "believe what you want, but I'm busy, so thank you and goodbye."

There's nothing I can do. He's a local big shot and I'm nobody with a big mouth. So I walk out.

En route, I spot the turtle, still sucking air in its tiny tank, staring at me with dull black eyes. I stop, turn and march back into the clinic. I'm not even sure why, but I'll find a reason.

"Still here?" says the vet, lounging in a chair.

"Ever been scuba diving?" I ask. He stares at me like I'm insane and starts to laugh.

"On my salary?" he replies. "Why do you ask?"

I jerk a thumb over my shoulder and say: "Because if you had, you'd see how turtles live. That tank is a disgrace. Call yourself a vet?"

His eyes pop. He rubs his stubbly chin, probably wondering how much anaesthetic to stick up my insolent arse.

"Anything else?" he asks, matter-of-factly. I get the impression he'd happily punch me in the nose. "Yes," I reply, "how much for your turtle?"

His assistant appears from behind a beaded curtain, with a worried look. He asks if everything is OK. The vet holds up his hand – *no problem.* He leans forward in his chair, rocking on his heels, thinking it over. Finally he says: "It's not for sale. It's mine."

"It should be in a lake," I suggest. "Plenty of lakes in Romania."

"It's not that kind of turtle," he explains.

For all I know about turtles, he's probably right.

"Oh," I reply, "so, I guess it's the kind of turtle that lives in a tank the size of a shoe-box, where it can't swim or turn round? And Bogdan's dopey dog chewed through two straps, right?"

He casts a glance towards the turtle sucking air on the ledge, among the plastic plants.

"If I put my turtle in a bigger tank," he asks mischievously, "would you be happy?"

"No," I reply, walking out. "But your turtle might."

Too Good to Be True

We start our hike at nine in the morning. The sun-dappled trail leads through thick woodland, up and up into Transylvania. It's hard but my guides are experienced and after two hours we emerge from the forest into rolling hills that soar above us for miles around. We stop to catch our breath. George hands me a plastic cup of ice cold water from a gurgling hole in the ground. The water tastes good, almost too good to be true. I'm in heaven, drinking angel beer. But is it wise?

"In Britain, it's not considered safe to drink from springs," I tell him, staring into the cup.

"In Romania, it's safe," says George, and we start walking. His wife Alina carries a huge rucksack of food and extra clothing but it seems no problem for her. I offer to swap because mine is a bit smaller, but she refuses.

"I'm used to it," she replies. Their young daughter Catrinel trots ahead or lags behind, depending how happy she is. It's tough being eight, at 2,000 meters. We are walking towards the glacial lake at Cindrel, south-west of Sibiu. It's about a 25 kilometre round trip, as the crow flies. But we don't have wings and the gradients are hellish steep.

George ties his hair back with a shoot of grass. Tanned and lean, he looks like a mountain man in his knee-length corduroy hiking pants, braces and stout boots. We soon rest again, this time at a rocky outcrop with a majestic view of Transylvania. I feel alive, lucky, tingling with wonder.

"I've loved these mountains since I was a kid," sighs George. A pair of crows ride the wind down into the valley then back up the other side, flung on a thermal breeze. It looks like fun. Alina points into the distance, at the huge green hill that awaits us.

"See up there, way up? That's where George and I first met, ten years ago," she says. Catrinel pulls at her mum's sleeve and murmurs something. Alina smiles and says:

"She wants to show you our rocks. Would you like to see them, Mike?"

"Rocks? Of course!"

"Good, let's go!"

We continue our walk and a little farther up the hill, George stops and looks around as if concerned, listening to the wind. He slips a bag of biscuits from his pack, passing me a handful.

"Thanks," I say, and start munching.

"They're not for you," he replies. Before I can get an explanation, three big dogs appear from nowhere, bounding towards us through deep grass, barking and snapping their teeth. They have wild eyes and thick fur. George tosses them a few biscuits. The dogs quieten down and gobble the goodies. Then they wait for more, their pink tongues hanging like slices of fresh ham.

"Feed them," George tells me, turning slowly. "Let them get your smell. Then walk after me, slowly. They'll follow, but don't worry, they won't bite. They're starving, not stupid."

I take his advice and we continue uphill, behind Alina and little Catrinel. I'm at the back. The sheepdogs follow us closely, jostling to be first. I can feel their hot breath on my bare calves.

After a hundred metres, we meet a shepherd. He looks like a scarecrow sticking up from the land, watching us approach. He wears a little black hat shaped like a bullet. It's made of rough felt. He has a face like a walnut, brown and wrinkled. He leans on a long pole of shaved white wood. He's about thirty years old. Or sixty, it's hard to tell.

"Hi," says George.

The shepherd nods and curls his lip. It could be a smile, it could be disdain. Or maybe he's just tired. One of the dogs circles us then lies down with a contented grunt, melding into the spongy grass. The other dogs lope away towards a big herd of sheep, a hundred strong, with thick grey wool daubed with big inky blotches, like school-kids have been colouring them in.

The shepherd looks a bit like Russell Crowe, with bright eyes that slant in the corners. He carries a yellow waterproof cape rolled up tight and a large plastic bottle which is half-full of tiny blueberries. His woolly sweater needs a wash, it clings to his scrawny frame. I expect a whiff of body odour from our weather-beaten wanderer, a knockout punch perhaps. But no, he smells of cut grass and wood-smoke. He turns to George.

"Do you have a cigarette?"

"Sorry, we don't smoke," says George. "Want some biscuits?" He offers a handful. The shepherd scoops them up. I give him two squares of dark chocolate. He raises an eyebrow.

"How long have you been up here?" George asks. The shepherd checks the sky, as if it might know.

"Since early May," he replies, matter-of-factly. It's early August. Three months of living rough. He wears old rubber Wellingtons. I feel a twinge of guilt in my big walking boots.

"Do you like your job?" I ask. He gives me a puzzled look. *Talk about a dumb question.*

"Yes", he replies, with a quick smile. "If I didn't, I wouldn't be here, right?"

He holds my gaze, waiting. I have a feeling our shepherd thinks I'm a bit soft in the head.

"Right," says George.

The sheepdog at our feet is missing half an ear. But it cannot be from a battle wound, because the edge is perfectly straight, as if someone cut it with a knife long ago. I point with my finger.

"Who cut his ear?" I ask.

"Me," says the shepherd, glancing at the dog. The dog raises its muzzle, suddenly alert.

"Why?" I ask.

"To make him fierce," says the shepherd. The dog looks up at me – *talk about a dumb answer.* Then it rolls over and closes its eyes to snooze in the sun.

"Seen any wolves?" asks George. Little Catrinel turns to listen. The shepherd shrugs.

"Plenty," he replies. "But I've only lost two sheep this summer. My dogs fight them off."

"Do they come at night?" asks Alina. The shepherd shakes his head, pops a blueberry.

"Just before dawn, when it's quiet. They're clever. They hide behind trees, waiting."

"We'd best be off," says George. The shepherd nods, as if giving permission. We rejoin our route uphill, following a dusty path across a vast green slope. The shepherd tramps away over a ridge and is swallowed by the land. I watch his little black hat dip into the grass, like a submarine sinking into a green ocean. He seems perfectly at ease in this wild and inhospitable spot, a son of the ancient soil. I'm suddenly struck by the difference between us. Out here, he is at home and at work. All he needs is a few dogs, a stick and a cigarette. The rest of us need offices and computers, cars and mobile phones.

I'm still thinking about it when we stop for lunch. We settle under a sturdy tree, take off our boots and dump our rucksacks, breathing hard. The sun is high and hot, but the wind keeps us cool. We take our rest, watching the blue sky where white clouds drift, fat and fluffy. We eat goat's cheese, green peppers, olives and crusty bread. The spring water in our bottle is still icy despite the midday heat. Rolling blue-green hills stretch for endless miles in each direction, as far as we can see. I feel lucky to be here. It's almost too good to be true.

"What happens if we get into trouble?" I ask. "Is there a rescue number we can phone?"

"No," says George. "This is considered a safe area. Up here, you're on your own."

He swishes long grass with a short stick. He seems very relaxed about that.

"What about wolves?" I ask. Little Catrinel glances up from her sandwich, wide-eyed.

"What about them?" sighs George, "If they're interested in you, forget it, you're already dead. But no need to worry in summer. They'd only attack us in winter, when they're starving and in a pack. Sheepdogs are worse, you never know with them. We were lucky, back there."

"Tell him about the German lady," murmurs Alina, as if she would rather not.

"A hiker," explains George. "Some sheepdogs attacked her on this same trail, almost ripped her guts out. Her friends ran back to Păltiniş to raise the alarm – took them two hours. Then someone fetched help from Sibiu. They finally got her to a hospital, lucky to survive."

"Who owned the dogs that attacked her?" I ask. "Didn't he get into trouble?"

"Are you kidding?" replies George. "Most shepherds don't give a damn about hikers."

The white clouds are turning grey above us. The wind is picking up. Change is in the air.

"But do you like our mountains?" asks Alina, looking around.

"Love them," I reply. "I've wanted to do this ever since George and I met, in ´95"

"So why didn't you?" inquires George. It's a good question. Eventually, I answer:

"Too busy doing things that seemed more important, I suppose."

George looks unconvinced by my alibi, and I don't blame him. He sighs and swishes his stick.

"*Life is what happens while you're making other plans*. John Lennon said that."

"I know," I reply. "I told you."

After lunch, we thread along a narrow path through low bushes laden with succulent wild blueberries – just like the shepherd's. We start picking and can't stop. They have a delicious tangy flavour and are doubtless packed with vitamin C. They are addictive too – we spend rather too long reaching high and low for the best clusters. By the time we move on we have full tummies, blue teeth and are grinning like vampires. Transylvania is too good to be true.

It is late afternoon. We walk across a hill strewn with dozens of shattered trees that lie at strange angles in the grass. It reminds me of something from TV news – the aftermath of a NATO attack? Dead grey branches poke from the ground like the bones of a huge dinosaur.

"What happened here?" I ask, surveying the scene.

"Lightning," says George. "There's some kind of metal underground, which attracts it."

"Quite a few people have been struck dead up here," adds Alina, matter-of-factly.

"Thanks for telling me," I reply.

It starts to rain, gently at first, just a few teasing drops. Alina checks the sky. She looks a little worried.

"We should go down," suggests George.

"Down?" I reply, disappointed. "It's only a bit of rain. Plus, we didn't see your rocks yet!"

"The weather turns quickly. . . " adds Alina. But Catrinel is tugging at her sleeve – *we must show him the rocks.* I pull out my waterproof top and brandish it with a determined grin. George and Alina smile ruefully at each other. They can't win. And off we go through shattered trees.

It doesn't take us long to find what we're looking for. Halfway across a bare expanse of rough grass, Alina raises her arm and points. One hundred meters away, I spy a jagged outcrop of rock. Shiny ledges of grey and black, layered like prehistoric cake, glistening under the light rainfall.

"That's them," says George, proudly. Catrinel runs ahead and skips up the rocks, nimble as a baby goat. She finds a toehold and strikes a pose for a photo. When we catch up, I gather the young family together for a portrait.

"George and I were hiking," explains Alina, settling her daughter on her knee, "with different groups of friends. We stopped here for a rest, at the same time, just by chance.

Catrinel likes that story. So every summer we come back. To sit on our rocks and stop for a rest!"

Catrinel grins. I click my button. A raindrop dribbles down my lens. I wipe it away and prepare to click again. But through the viewfinder, I notice George is no longer looking at the camera. He's looking upwards. Ominous-looking clouds appear over the hills, rolling towards us. Bad news and travelling fast. He appears increasingly concerned. Alina catches his eye and seems to agree. Sure enough, the wind begins to whistle around our heads and soon two huge black clouds are drawing closer together, low in the sky, like celestial armies on the eve of battle. George extricates himself from the happy huddle and slides down from the rocks.

"We must find shelter," he announces firmly, twisting to help Catrinel. "Come on!"

The nearest option is a dense forest, 1,000 meters back down the way we came. George sets a quick pace with long strides, trotting more than walking. Somewhere in the distance, a dog begins to bark. Alina and George exchange worried glances.

"We should hurry," she advises.

The rain falls harder. Clouds flash and rumble. We're halfway across the hill of dead trees when a fork of silver lightning scythes into the ground with an almighty crack, 50 meters ahead of us. The air booms like a massive bomb just exploded. We jump in fright. It's the loudest bang I have ever heard. The grass hisses and steams, marking the spot. Nobody speaks. We just stand and stare, mesmerized by the awesome power of nature. Our pleasant walk in the hills is suddenly a race between life and death. We start running.

"Come on!" yells George, heading down towards the big forest beyond. But it seems miles away and we are sitting ducks, at the mercy of the gods. The sky roars vengeance as we jog through thick wet grass that snatches at our heels.

Voices come to us on the wind. I spot dark shapes in a small valley nearby, through the driving rain. People are running for cover among ragged huts, like poor ranchers in a cowboy film. They wear bullet-shaped hats, same as our shepherd. George spins around, shouting as he runs.

"Dogs! Watch out!"

"What?!" cries Alina, pulling her daughter close. Catrinel's skinny little legs are pumping like pistons in her sodden jeans as we scurry down the hill towards the woods. But the dogs have seen us, we're not going to make it. I can hear them barking like crazy. Then I see them in the distance: four or five, with dark pointy ears bobbing through deep grey grass to our left. I shove a hand into my pocket for some biscuits: all gone. The scene takes on a dreamy quality, as if I'm not really here. I think of the German hiker, guts ripped open. I have no stick, no chance. I'm at the back of our group. The dogs will reach me first. The sky explodes above us. Heavy rain batters at my head. I sense my body preparing itself for trauma and pain.

George screams at the shepherds, but in vain. They are too busy sheltering from the storm and don't hear us. Or they don't care. Their dogs are 20 meters away from us, gaining fast. The first one looks like a hound from hell, big and black, with snapping jaws. The other dogs are smaller but look equally vicious. They have mottled coats, grey-brown. One is snowy white. We are strangers on their territory. We are in trouble. Here they come.

The pack of five suddenly splits. Two dogs run left to block our progress. Three run right, to block any retreat. We slow down, surrounded. The dogs close in, legs splayed, eyes aflame, crouching and barking and slavering, teeth exposed like ivory daggers.

Suddenly, from nowhere, a barefoot kid scampers down the hill brandishing a huge stick. He yells at the dogs. They freeze, panting and glaring at us. The kid jabs his stick towards a gap in the circle of hackled fur and gives us the nod. We walk towards the gap then run.

"Thank God!" yells George, over his shoulder.

The dogs bark back: *Go to Hell!*

We reach the woods and don't stop running until we are deep inside, where raindrops clatter through the branches and slither down our necks like winners' medals. We splash through puddles and slip on muddy leaves as the gloom finally engulfs us. Thunder and lightning continue high overhead, but the gods have other fish to fry. We are safe. We pause, panting for breath.

Our eyes are glowing, our faces pale with shock. We don't look back.

Back Door Man

I'm wearing a tie and a smile. It's my first day. But the security guard won't let me in, *because-because.* I stand in the entrance of the Ministry, pleading. The guard reads an SMS, smiling down at his mobile. Then he looks up and stares at me, if as if I'm not right in the head.

"What?" he asks.

A guy in a suit trots up the marble steps and breezes through with a cursory wave of a white plastic card. I ask the Security guy how I can get one. He frowns and replies:

"You can't."

I point to the elevator, ten yards across the spacious lobby, near a big bonsai tree.

"See that lift?" I explain, "That's the one I used when they hired me. I'm not a terrorist. I'm on contract, helping the Ministry."

He gives me a dark look:

"Terrorist?"

I shake my head and say:

"Consultant."

"*Domnul,*" he responds, with a shrug, "only Ministers, Heads of Department and other important people use the front door."

"I know," I reply. "They brought me through it last week! Don't you remember? Please, can you let me in? I have a meeting at nine, I'll be late! Please?" He considers it, like the final question on a TV quiz, like he'll win $64,000 if he gets it right.

"Back door," he replies, prodding his phone.

I walk around the rear of the building, searching. Finally I spot a grubby steel entrance with brown paint peeling. I glance up, half-expecting to see a big sign for Plebs. I snake my way inside, ask directions and find the lobby, back where I started. The same guard waves to me, old friends now.

"OK?" he asks. I wonder how to reply. But the lift doors open, so I don't have to.

Five floors up, the meeting room has wood-panelled walls, comfy chairs, a big oval table and a view of Bucharest's skyline. Five guys in suits sit around, puffing hard on cigarettes. The place is thick with smoke. One guy sighs as if it's 5 pm on Friday, not 9 am on Monday. They glance at me like we're all members of a jury on a complex case we don't understand. They all have white plastic cards around their neck or tagged to their lapels. I ask why.

"So we can use the front door," one of them replies, rubbing his eyes. He looks tired. "How I can get one?" I ask.

"You can't," he replies.

"The front door is only for us," mutters another, stubbing out a cigarette.

"Why?" I ask. "We all use the same lift and we come to the same room. So why can't we use the same door? Plus, it's a bit of a trek around the back..."

But nobody answers. At 9.40 am the boss enters, laughing into his mobile phone. He sits down at the head of the table and tells me he did not like my predecessor.

"Because he was patronizing and treated us like second-class citizens."

I write it down.

I Will Never Leave Romania

Vera is charming, articulate and witty. A little bossy perhaps, but it makes me want to please her.

"Think about it," she advises, in a perfect English accent. She sounds like she's from Buckinghamshire, not Bucharest. She gets up from our small table in the corner of the busy tea shop and strides across the parquet floor towards the washrooms, like a headmistress in search of naughty boys. Our mutual friend Lumi leans forward with twinkling eyes and asks:

"Happy?"

"Happy?" I reply, "I can hardly believe my ears. Thank you for the introduction."

Because Vera works in publishing. She even likes my stories and says they should be in a book. She'll talk to her boss. And there's something else – she sympathizes with my theory that some of my Romanian friends have become a little unhinged, schizophrenic even, over the years.

"Or maybe it's me?" I suggest, when Vera returns. She shakes her head.

"This country is changing and people are changing with it," she confides. "I like how you write about that, as an outsider. It's interesting to hear your perspective. Tell me more."

So I tell her about Doctor Mihai who agreed to buy my old car but changed the price once I gave him the keys. Or Bogdan, who screamed at me about how Clinton bombed Serbia to destabilize the euro, told me to *f*** off* when I disagreed. Or my clever dentist who hates Jews because-because. Or smart Anna who says feeding a hungry dog causes rabies. Or Cătă, who has turned into a designer-yuppie and drives his Porsche at Mach 2 through impoverished villages. Or Mariana, who welcomed me like a long-lost son but then chewed my ear off when I suggested she might try a little *please* and *thank you* with the waiter in my local pizzeria.

Vera listens keenly, like I'm clever or something. I tell her I blame communism.

"It took away their role models," I suggest. "What do you think?"

Vera doesn't reply. She just peers at me over her specs, like a prim librarian, too clever to help.

"But you know what?" I continue, "Romanians who work abroad seem to cope better. I know because I've met them, all over the place. Their horizons widen. Maybe that's the answer?"

"Not for me," replies Vera, firmly. "I will never leave Romania. It's my home, it has a subtle culture. All my friends are here. I want to make it a better place. I'm rooted, I'm staying!"

"Good for you," I reply, "Romania is one big boomtown, lots of potential for you."

Not to mention me, if she keeps her word. Vera smiles knowingly, like she can read my mind.

"And who knows," she adds, with a sigh, "if I publish your stories. . . "

I'm glowing all over. I want to hug her, make babies, build a cottage on a hill. Lumi tells me to calm down. I promise to write more. Vera says *yes indeed*, she'll need lots for the book.

By now we've been waiting forty minutes, but at last the smiling waitress in the low-cut top brings us an elegant teapot and three white china cups. People without seats cluster at the door and watch us with baleful eyes – *hurry-up-and-drink-it.* So we do, making plans.

A few days later, I meet Lumi in the elevator of our block. I mention Vera, whether she got my recent email with my latest story. Lumi grins like she has good news.

"Yes, Vera phoned last night! She loves it! She says you've inspired her to write! She read it on the plane to Brussels. Oh, and guess what else? She resigned from her job! She's going to become an EU interpreter! She isn't coming back, but we mustn't tell her dad."

Lumi stops and looks concerned, staring at me. Then she leans closer and says:

"Mike, are you OK?"

People from Bucharest

We reach our destination at 6 pm. We are high in the hills of Transylvania, 25 kilometers south-west of Sibiu. The land undulates all around us in grey-blue waves, like an ocean. There is no sound except for birdsong on a breeze. I have wanted to walk these peaks and valleys since my first visit to Romania in 1994. The land I stumbled on by accident. The land I now call home. Somehow, events and schedules and obligations have always conspired against me. But today, finally, I have time. I'm back in Transylvania: the heart of the nation, some say.

I gaze around me, trying to imagine the countless individuals who have trekked these hills over the millennia: warriors and shepherds, peasants and poets. I feel warm, optimistic and completely knackered after an nine-hour hike through sun and rain. But I made it. Along with my long-time buddy George, his wife Alina and little Catrinel, eight years-old and keen as mustard.

The Cănaia mountain refuge sits 50 meters before us, halfway up a long steep hill, with dense woodland below and grassy slopes above. It is a low building made of stone with a tin roof that shines like gold-leaf in the dying sun. We are relieved that we will have a bed for the night. Except maybe we won't. Because, on closer inspection, we discover that the best room in the refuge is already occupied and the others look like exhibits in a run-down folk museum. Big rusty padlocks prevent us checking for alternatives.

We sit outside on a knoll, assessing our options. Alina holds her head in her hands then glances sideways at her husband.

"We screwed up, George," she says. He shrugs and watches little Catrinel walk downhill, pigtails bouncing, towards the outdoor toilet, "You won't like it, Catrinel," he yells.

Sure enough Catrinel opens the broken door of the toilet then yelps and runs back to us, holding her nose.

"This place has turned into a real dump," sighs George.

"You mentioned another refuge?" I say.

"Twelve kilometers away," he replies, "too late now."

Catrinel scampers to her mum and garbles a report on the stinky loo. The sun dips over one horizon and a dark fuzzy line rises towards us from the other. Night is creeping upon us, inch by inch. The dense canopy of woodland below changes gradually from bright green to dark grey. The warm air begins to chill.

"Hear about that American hiker?" asks Alina. But it's no joke, and we know it.

"Killed by a bear," I reply, "because he couldn't find a place in a refuge."

Alina lies back with both hands behind her head, looking up at the darkening Transylvanian sky. She turns to us and speaks quietly.

"I read in a newspaper that the bear was angry because the hiker took a photo with a flash."

The wind whispers to the trees, as if spreading the latest gossip. After a moment, George replies.

"What, they interviewed the bear?"

It raises a laugh, but not our hopes. A torchlight flashes inside the refuge and a ghostly face appears at a window. George gets up and ambles towards the building, bowlegged in his big boots, brown calves shining in the twilight.

"Let me talk to these guys," he suggests, "see if they can help."

Little Catrinel finds a stick and pokes at a hole in the tufted grass. It's what sticks are for.

"We haven't used this refuge in four years," Alina tells me. "These days we sleep in a three-man tent. But seeing as there are four of us on this trip, I didn't bring it."

It sounds like a logical decision, but maybe it wasn't. We could've squeezed in.

When George reappears, he's rubbing his hands together and seems pleased with himself.

"We're in luck! Those kids inside know the old guy who runs this place. He gave them keys to the best rooms. Guess what, there's another room and it's not too bad! Come and see!"

We follow George up the rickety wooden steps into the refuge. In the stone-floored lobby, four teenagers sit around a table: three lads, one of whom has a doe-eyed girl perched on his knee. Her arms drape around his shoulders like this is their last night together, or maybe their first. The four youngsters watch us through cigarette smoke and we exchange brief greetings.

George leads us down the corridor to an open door, where a rusty padlock now hangs loose. The room beyond contains three battered metal cots that sag in the middle. It's not the Ritz, but it's better than nestling in a tree. George strides about like a proud home-owner.

"Seems the old guy who runs this place has a sick wife, that's why he's not here."

Absent, but conscientious: the white walls look freshly-painted and thick blankets sit neatly-folded on a wooden stool. I run my fingers over them – not too damp, we should be OK.

"Catrinel can jump in with me," suggests Alina. "She likes that."

Catrinel grins at her mother – *you bet.*

Outside, night has fallen. We sit around the campfire in woolly sweaters, listening to jokes from the teenage hikers. The two lads squat by the fire, trading insults and tossing wood into the flames from a stack of neatly cut blocks. Before long, the fire roars and blazes. They have a two-litre bottle of beer but they don't share it with us. Nearby, the two lovers peck and coo each other like a pair of pigeons. High above our fire, an aircraft drones through the night. I look up and watch its tiny winking lights, wondering if the passengers can see our red-hot dot.

"Why don't you talk to Mike? He's from England," suggests George. He sounds a bit like the host of a party who goes around telling guests to get up and dance, *have some fun*.

"What about?" asks Sami, who seems to be the leader of the four teenagers. He does most of the talking and always has the final word. He's short and dark, with boyish good looks, wide sloping shoulders and sturdy legs like a footballer. Shy Dinu is his perfect foil: tall and fair, with bright blue eyes and a shock of blonde hair, a true son of Saxony. The two young lovers meanwhile remain in the shadows, whispering and giggling.

"Are you at school, or working?" I ask. Sami smiles, like only he knows the answer.

"Military college in Sibiu," he replies, puffing up his chest.

"Good for you," I say, impressed. "Romanian soldiers get deployed all over the world."

"Not quite," says Sami, gazing up at the first stars. His buddy Dinu laughs, quietly.

"Well, they're in Congo, Bosnia, Iraq, Afghanistan..." I reply.

"But that's not the whole world, is it?" asks Sami.

Dinu laughs again. Sami digs him with his elbow. I get the impression they're a double act, the life and soul of every teenage party in Sibiu, when they get invited. But after a long day's hiking, I'm too tired for a battle of wits.

"Well, perhaps they're not at the North Pole," I reply. But Sami doesn't seem interested.

"So, what's after military college?" asks George. Sami shrugs.

"Special Forces or IT," he replies, adding quickly, "but probably Special Forces." He stares glassy-eyed at the fire. I can just see him in a swamp with a dagger between his teeth.

"And how about you, Dinu?" asks Alina, hugging her knees.

"Theatre school," replies Dinu. "I juggle, sing songs, play piano."

"So you'll be in Special Forces too?" I suggest. Sami hoots with laughter and barks:

"No chance!"

"Seriously, Dinu, what would you like to do after theatre school?" I ask.

"Masters," replies Dinu, brimming with confidence. Sami shakes his head in disbelief. Presumably he'd prefer to be blowing things up. "Then probably my PhD," adds Dinu.

"Wow, then what?" says Alina. Dinu stares back at her, as if nobody asked him before. He seems stuck for an answer. "I mean what job?" adds Alina, helpfully.

"Are you kidding?" chuckles Sami. "He's a professional student, this one!"

"Not true!" scowls Dinu. "I'll play in a jazz band maybe, travel the world. I want to be a musician. Last week I watched a DVD of *The Piano,* 26 times in 3 days."

Sami looks at Dinu and then at us. He rolls his eyes, evidently unimpressed.

"Do you need a PhD to play in a jazz band?" I ask.

"I just want to make people happy," he replies, finally. Our fire cracks and hisses. Dinu stands over it for a few moments, kicking at the edges. Then he picks up a large axe and disappears into the darkness, leaving us to fathom his logic. After a few moments we hear the crunch of steel on wood, a few yards away. I'm wondering why. We don't need wood, because there's already a large pile of neatly-cut blocks by the fire. Perhaps he's making a piano.

Sami sips beer from the big plastic bottle and passes it to the two lovebirds. George produces a small bottle of vodka and offers it around. The three teenagers drink deeply and pass it back, almost empty. George watches in polite silence and shares the last sip with his wife. Little Catrinel is nodding off on a red blanket. Sami smacks his lips, puffs up his chest and says:

"So?"

He seems to be ready for more questions, or more vodka.

"Do you like living in Sibiu?" I ask.

"Better than living in Bucharest!" he replies, grinning at me through the flames. His eyes flicker red, like coals. He flashes a glance at the lovers. They nod at him in agreement. The girlfriend is chewing her hair. The boyfriend kisses the top of her head. She looks up at him with a sweet smile like they're going to stay together for ten years, or at least ten days.

"You don't like Bucharest?" I ask. Sami shakes his head. His tanned face glows orange in the firelight like a pumpkin at Halloween.

"No, we don't," says the boyfriend, breaking his silence.

"Why not?" I ask.

Sami groans – it's clearly a dumb question.

"People from Bucharest are arrogant," he says. "They drive up here in their big cars and they think they know it all."

It's a familiar provincial complaint that could be heard in any country. But here and now, his youthful scorn burns brighter than our fire.

"Do you agree?" I ask the girlfriend. She runs a hand through her hair.

"Yes," she replies sleepily. "People from Bucharest are very loud and have no manners. They're not real Romanians. The Turks infiltrated them. We're different, in Transylvania."

Big blond Dinu returns from the darkness dragging a short narrow tree trunk. He quickly hacks off some branches and thrusts them onto the embers. The wood hisses but does not burn.

"Green wood," observes George. "Young tree, it wasn't dead."

"It is now," replies Dinu, tossing the axe into the night. Then he slumps to the ground. George looks at me in baffled silence and shakes his head – *the kid's a fool.*

"Hey, Dinu, what do you think of people from Bucharest?" I ask.

"I don't," he replies, rubbing muck from his hands.

"Are they too smart-ass, too *şmecheri*?" I say, hoping the slang will open him up. It does.

"*Şmecheri*, exactly. Big ideas, big mouths, big deal!"

Dinu and Sami slap a hi-five. The teenage lovebirds giggle in unison, then rise to their feet and disappear towards the refuge arm-in-arm, two dark shapes wobbling up the grassy hill. The tin roof glints silver under the stars. The old wooden door creaks and they vanish inside.

"Full moon," sighs Alina, looking up, her throat as white as a midnight swan.

"It looks rusty," adds little Catrinel, with a tiny yawn. She's got a point. We sit listening to Sami and Dinu's beery wisdom until they start slurring their words. I take a pee in the bushes nearby. When I get back, George and his family are striding towards the refuge, on stiff legs.

In a few minutes we lie under musty blankets in our chilly room. To keep warm, I'm still fully-dressed. My bed is perhaps the most uncomfortable I have ever slept in, much damper than I expected. I feel vaguely wet all over. Despite the dead silence, I am so accustomed to brakes screeching every night in Bucharest that I swear I can hear some even here. But no, I'm in deepest Transylvania, 2,224 m above sea-level. Finally, the nine hours of hard hiking take their toll and I'm soon sliding over a rocky abyss into a warm and welcoming place. The last thing I hear is George muttering *this country is going to the dogs.* He sounds fed up, but I'm too busy with my sheep to care.

We're back on the trail by eight the next morning, trekking up grey-green slopes that rise like tidal waves before us. The walk gets easier and soon we are strolling happily across a wide plateau and joking about a game of football. Then another surprise: the land suddenly dips at an angle of 45 degrees. It's hair-raising. Below us, at the bottom of the slope, sits a perfect post-glacial lake, like water in a saucer: *Lacul Iezerul Mare.* It shimmers under the mid-morning sun. Bushes protrude from the sheer rock above, like blotches of green paint daubed by a child.

"My lake," announces George. Alina threads her arm around his waist.

"Actually, it's *our* lake," she says, pulling little Catrinel closer to them. We scramble down the slope and dump our heavy backpacks. We take off our boots and paddle in ice-cold water, clapping hands for an echo.

"Swim?" I ask, hoping nobody will agree.

"If you want a heart attack," replies George. "Happens every year, to city guys usually!"

"Because their blood is too hot after hiking," explains Alina. "And the water is too cold."

Nearby we find the charred remains of a campfire, still warm from recent visitors. Doubtless they were people who love natural beauty and solitude; people who hiked all day then slept in a tent; people who left their empty beer cans, plastic bottles and food wrappers strewn in a wide circle.

"Who would do such a thing?" asks George, surveying the mess.

"People from Bucharest?" suggests Alina ironically, as she lays out a picnic lunch.

"People from Mars," adds George. Catrinel giggles and chews a chunk of white cheese.

We arrive back in the resort village of Păltiniş a few hours later, down the valley. We board a mud-spattered bus for the ride home to Sibiu. It's full of teenagers. Most of them are wearing muddy boots after a day on the hills. But some wear slinky tops and spotless Adidas trainers, for a night on the town. We move along the central aisle, looking for vacant seats.

"Hey, George!" shouts a familiar voice. It's Sami, full of beans, with deep grey rings under his eyes. He leans from his seat in the middle of the bus, hand in the air to slap a hi-five. But George keeps his hands in his pockets as we pass. He nods at Sami and at Dinu who is sitting nearby, taking up two seats, big and blond and fiddling with a mobile phone. Farther back, the two teenage lovebirds are still holding onto each other. I begin to wonder if they ever let go.

I greet the four teenage hikers and keep walking towards empty seats near the back. The doors hiss and swing shut. The engine rumbles, the bus pulls away. Catrinel starts drawing stick men in the steamy windows. Alina snuggles beside her young daughter to draw a big daisy. George doesn't look very happy. I sit in the empty seat beside him, curious.

"What's up?" I ask, in a low voice.

"Remember the beer they were drinking last night? They stole it."

"What?"

"They bust open the cupboards, the beer was inside. It belonged to the old guy who runs the refuge, the one who gave them the keys to the best rooms. With the sick wife, remember?"

I can hardly believe my ears. It's quite an accusation, tumbling like crockery from a cupboard.

"Says who?" I ask.

"Sami! Last night, just before bed, I forgot to tell you," murmurs George, looking pissed off. *This country is going to the dogs.*

Now I get it. That's why George was fed up at bedtime. He also kept it quiet today, on our way down. Didn't want to spoil our walk? Now he's spitting fire.

"They burned all his wood, too. I spotted that this morning. Who would do such things?"

"People from Bucharest?" I suggest, ironically. George turns and smiles, but not really.

We watch Sami and his buddy. Tinny music fills the coach from Dinu's phone. He kneels in his seat and cranks up the volume, whether the rest of us like turbo-folk *manele* music or not. The scratchy violins and shrill flutes sound like fingernails down a blackboard. He starts singing along, yelling to someone farther down the coach. Most of the other passengers don't seem too interested in Dinu, but he seems determined to make us all happy. That's all he wants to do.

Sami leans out and yells down the aisle.

"Hey, driver! Close this damn window above my head, there's a draught!"

The window slides shut. Sami watches it, like a kid at a magic show. Then he sinks back into his seat and raises his knees, wedging himself into a more comfortable position. In front, a young woman is reading a paperback. Or rather, she was. She turns around into the aisle and glares at Sami. She doesn't seem happy having his kneecaps in her spine. He shrugs and says:

"What's your problem?"

She turns away without a word.

George shakes his head at me in mute despair and lets out a long sigh. He stares off through our window. He wipes condensation and watches dense woodland rushing by. A lorry loaded with construction material passes us, coated with a fine grey patina of cement dust.

"Romania is changing," he remarks. "And it's not all good."

Then the bus stops and fills with more passengers – country folk with leathery faces and threadbare clothes. Their fingers are brown and knobbly like wood. Grimy flip-flops curl around their woollen socks like old bread. They clamber aboard to stand wherever they find a place. Some sit on the muddy steps, staring at their feet. The bus seems about to burst. Most of our new passengers look wet and exhausted, as if they've spent a long hard day in some rainy, godforsaken field. Their torn bags bulge with vegetables. Dinu's music tinkles overhead.

The air gradually turns fetid. It soon stinks of cow shit, body odour, garlic and stale alcohol. Soon I begin to feel I cannot breathe. Little Catrinel pinches her nose between thumb and finger. Alina whispers in her ear. Catrinel removes her hand and presses her nose to the window, making steamy circles. Someone shouts to the driver. The bus slows and stops. One of the farm workers hops off, covered in muck. As he departs, he says in a loud voice:

"It stinks in here."

Then he's gone, and so are we, down a long road of new tarmac that glistens in the rain.

Travel Broadens the Mind

The taxi driver drops me at Băneasa Airport, on the edge of Bucharest, and charges 17 lei. It's a fair price. I sling my rucksack over one shoulder and walk towards the domed building. It looks like something from a 1950's sci-fi comic – half a giant grapefruit turned upside down. They say it will be refurbished soon, but I like that retro styling. As usual, the narrow entrance lobby is crammed with people. It's hot. Some of them are in a hurry, sweating and looking worried. Most just seem bored with waiting. I edge through, register at the desk and walk down the slope to the departure area.

It's crowded, far busier than I remember, far too small for the number of passengers. We deserve better. People are packed together on plastic seats, leaning against the walls or sitting cross-legged on the floor: kids with cute knapsacks and dollies; muscle-bound dudes in tight vests, reading car magazines; a middle-aged couple nibbling sandwiches; an old guy in a Ceauşescu safari suit, watching the world through horn-rimmed spectacles with violet lenses.

Some passengers cluster around the departure doors in amorphous huddles, clutching their tickets and snacks, keen to be first on the plane. Beyond the smoked glass, bright green fields stretch flat to the horizon like a calm lagoon. Aircraft come and go, engines screaming. After a forty-minute wait, my flight to Luton is announced. Some passengers who arrived late now sneak in front of the crowd, trying not to be noticed. They affect blank expressions and stare ahead to avoid eye contact. It seems to work. Nobody complains.

On board our plane, the central aisle is soon blocked by a dozen passengers, all leisurely stashing their bags and arguing about who will sit where. Dozens more – including me – are waiting to get to our seats. But we can't, because Aurel-wants-to-sit-with-Maria-but-Bogdan-has-to-go-by-the-window. They seem completely oblivious to the rest of us. Some other Romanians get fed up waiting and try to push past, which triggers a fierce argument and only makes things worse. A hostess on the intercom requests the slow passengers to make way. But they don't. It takes them a few minutes to resolve their problems and finally sit down, laughing among themselves.

The plane fills up and glamorous hostesses sashay down the aisle in red hats, checking that we are all buckled in. Two beefy men to my right seem unhappy about wearing seat belts, but a hostess explains that this is for their own safety. She points a big red fingernail at the little red light and tells them to keep their belts on until the bulb turns green, because that's the law. But by now the two men are flicking through an in-flight magazine, checking the booze prices.

"Did you hear me?" asks the hostess. They glance up – *hear what?* The plane taxis and takes off. As soon as we are airborne, the two men unclip their belts with a noisy *clack* and toss the straps aside, flexing their broad backs. We are still soaring into the clouds but the sound acts as a signal to everyone else. Moments later the entire cabin echoes with a dull metallic clacking as more and more passengers unhook their belts. A voice on the intercom asks people to put their belts back on. Nobody seems to be listening.

The flight is quiet until drinks are served. Then a big guy in front orders two cans of Heineken and reclines his seat to the max. Soon he is yapping at the top of his voice, rocking back and forth like a rodeo rider, telling tall tales. I feel like I'm on a school trip – we're all twelve and going to the zoo, or something. The guy gets to his punch-line and thrusts his hand behind his head, almost poking my eye out. The handsome Romanian woman sitting next to me says:

"Watch out."

We chat and I offer her some dried apricots. She's aged about forty, well-dressed in a suit and pearls. Her English accent is excellent. She's from Craiova but lives in London, works in computers, has a British boyfriend. It's his company. She didn't like it at first, but does now.

"Because England is so different," she says, with a sigh.

"How?" I inquire. She watches fluffy clouds. She seems to be thinking. Finally she says:

"It just is."

We flick through the in-flight magazine, discussing destinations and low-cost flights.

"Life is different now, we can go anywhere!" she says, happily. But she sounds a bit sad too, as if her discoveries are tinged with regret, like a kid who just saw the neighbour's new toys.

As soon as we land in the UK, half a dozen people jump from their seats, grab their bags and stand in the aisle. The plane is still taxiing along the runway. The woman from Craiova smiles at me and whispers:

"This happens all the time, like they're on a bus!" A hostess voice comes on the intercom and asks everyone to sit down. Nobody does. Moments later the hostess walks down the aisle and orders people back to their seats. The naughty passengers obey, but reluctantly.

It feels odd to be back in the UK after so long. Riding to the terminal, I remember my last trip – two years ago, dad's funeral? Hopefully, this will be a happier visit. As we enter the hall, I notice more police than before, all dressed like paratroopers and bristling with weapons. But the atmosphere is quiet and calm, just another day in the UK, with miserable weather for free.

In the queue for passport control, I spot a young Romanian from my flight, wearing rosary beads and ragged jeans. He keeps glancing around, as if checking on something. Then he bends down, slips underneath the security tape and joins a shorter queue. He grins at his mates.

"SIR!" booms a male voice. Heads turn. A stocky British guy in a grey blazer strides towards us across the vinyl floor, gripping a walkie-talkie. He's short and serious-looking, with a military gait. A laminated ID card is clipped to his lapel. He jabs a podgy finger at the smartass in the shades and barks at him, short and sharp.

"You, go back behind the tape! That's why it's there!"

The Romanian dude retreats meekly and ducks under the security tape. He shrugs at his giggling mates – *who, me?* The stocky Brit walks away, checking left and right, vigilant.

At the luggage reclaim I sit on a trolley, watching and waiting from a distance. Most of the passengers from my flight crowd around the conveyor belt, three deep, elbow-to-elbow as they watch the circling bags with worried faces. Nobody else can get close until they are done.

A month later, I fly from Romania to Paris on another cheap flight. The routine is exactly the same: in the departure hall, latecomers push to the front of the queue; other Romanians frown but nobody protests. On the plane, a handful of passengers fuss and block the aisle; some complain about the seat belts and discard them moments after we are airborne. In the arrivals hall, a young wise-guy ducks under the tape and waves at his leggy girlfriend to follow suit.

"Come on!" he hisses – *nobody saw me*. Perhaps he's forgotten that there are a hundred fellow-passengers watching from a few yards away. Some Romanians shake their heads in disapproval. At the luggage belt, people crowd at the small steel circle, blocking their compatriots and everyone else. I sit and watch, wondering why. Don't they trust each other?

In the bus-bay, we wait for the shuttle into Paris city centre. Most of the Romanians smoke as soon as possible, sucking hard on their cigarettes with anxious faces, desperate for their fix. Our driver is a big black guy, who marches around with a clipboard. He opens the luggage hold and invites us to stash our bags underneath. Some people don't seem to understand. They stand back, as if expecting him to do it for them. He walks off, saying:

"That's your job, not mine."

Finally they get the idea, grab their bags and toss them haphazardly into the hold. The driver reappears, bends down and stares inside. He doesn't look happy. He quickly rearranges the bags, shaking his head. On the bus, waiting to go, everyone is chatting excitedly until he walks down the central aisle, checking numbers with a pencil. He's huge, like a grizzly bear. Everyone goes quiet, dead silent as he passes, counting heads.

The engine starts with a quiet rumble and soon we are purring along silky highways where drivers indicate before overtaking and yield at roundabouts. Nobody beeps their horn. I watch some of my fellow travellers. They are staring through the tinted windows in silence.

At Heathrow, a few weeks later, the flight to Bucharest is delayed by two hours. The boarding queue is over a hundred yards long. Why? Because that's life at Heathrow – a national disgrace, ask any Brit. Three hundred people stand quietly in line, reading or staring at the walls. Bored kids dangle from their parents, asking *mummy-why, daddy-what*. A large guy in a dark suit and shiny shoes marches to the front of the line to argue with the slim security woman. She wears a blue shirt, walkie-talkie and no make-up. She tries to calm him down. He's not listening.

"I must get home – now!" he bellows in broken English.

"Sir, the flight to Bucharest is delayed," she replies. But the man in the suit keeps on complaining, waving his arms up and down, brandishing his rolled-up copy of the FT and turning in circles like a ballet dancer on top of a music box. He looks as if he has lost his mind.

"Please join the back of the queue", says the security woman, pointing. He turns around and ogles the long line of tired travellers, including me. He has baggy eyes and looks unhappy.

"The back?!" he wails, like a kid who's lost his mum. "Do you know who I am?!"

The security woman studies him for a moment. He seems deflated when she replies:

"No, sir, I do not."

In Rome's Fiumicino Airport, fifty passengers wait quietly in a long curving line for the Bucharest flight. Everyone looks tanned and wears bright summer clothes. Some carry bags from the glittering Duty Free. People chat in Romanian, French, Italian, English and some languages I don't recognize. It's nice to be in Italy in July, with all the other nations. I'm near the front of the line, feeling calm and relaxed after a long weekend with an old friend. I'm watching the two Italian ladies behind the desk. They have beautiful eyes with long lashes. They wear stylish, see-through linen blouses. They have perfect hair and make-up. Best of all they have lovely voices, and seem to sing rather than talk. I could listen to Italian all day. It's like the opera, no charge.

After about forty minutes, a group of five latecomers arrive – four young guys in bright T-shirts and gelled hair, with a heavily-pregnant blonde woman aged about thirty. I'm close enough to hear what happens. The guy leading the group plops five Romanian passports on the counter.

"We want to board," he announces, "my wife is pregnant."

"We're not boarding yet, sir," replies one of the elegant ladies behind the desk.

"Well, we have to go first. She's pregnant. Look, can't you see?" He jerks a thumb at the blonde woman, who obliges with a wince and a smile. The Italian official replies:

"Sir, when we board you can go ahead with her, but not your three friends. See the queue? Some people have been here an hour, so please go to the back and…"

But he just shakes his head.

"She's *pregnant*," he says, louder, "and we're all together." The Italian lady ignores him. After a moment, he gives up and turns away to tell his wife. She folds her arms and rolls her eyes. The three men waiting with her swap horrified glances, as if they'll never see each other again. One throws his hands in the air, moaning as if he is the victim of an international plot. But they don't join the queue. They just stay where they are, chatting amongst themselves and comparing passports. Some of the Romanians in the queue glare at them. French *dames* in silk scarves exchange glances. German kids look up at their mums, hoping they might explain.

Weeks later, in the airport at Zurich, I spot a tight phalanx of four muscled men hulking towards me in a shopping mall. They wear police uniforms and are guarding a tall dark skinny guy who walks between them. His hair is gelled into spikes. He has no luggage, just bags of attitude. He wears a crisp white shirt, a glittery belt looped through tight white jeans, and white patent leather shoes with pointy toes. He struts along, rolling his shoulders and chewing gum. His eyes are hidden behind wraparound mirror shades. He looks like a pop star. People turn to watch.

Later, in the queue for the flight back to Bucharest, a handsome young man behind me is yapping loudly on his mobile in Italian. His hair is slicked back, black stubble covers his jaw and he wears an expensive-looking linen suit. But there is something rather unconvincing about the way he behaves. He's like an actor performing for everyone in the queue, including myself. He keeps glancing sideways at us, smiling and fluttering his eyes, as if inviting complete strangers to share his dilemma. I notice a trio of young women, staring at him. Their hair is coiled into dreadlocks. They have battered rucksacks with sleeping rolls on top. Paperback novels poke from the side pockets – students on their gap year perhaps. They exchange puzzled looks. One of them seems to be trying not to laugh at the flashy guy in the suit. I'm wondering why until he spins on his heel, turning his back towards me. He stands yapping into his phone, admiring his glossy shoes. Then I spot what the girls must have spotted: he has a yellow Post-It note stuck to his back on which someone has written in big letters, with a felt pen, in English: *I'M A ROMANIAN GIGOLO*.

As our plane takes off, the Swiss countryside is swallowed in thick mist until only round tree-tops are visible, floating like green jellyfish across waves of grey. During the flight back to Bucharest, the old man next to me hogs the window, his bald head silhouetted like an egg against bright sun. He keeps jerking back and forth, checking the horizon, as if he can't quite believe he is flying. I feel glad for him but his movement creates a strobe effect on my book, until I feel I'm going to be sick. In front, to my left, a teenage girl is chatting loudly across the aisle in Romanian to a young guy in front of me. I give up reading and close my eyes.

After a few minutes of sleep, I feel a sharp jab in my left foot. I look up and notice that the teenage girl is now straddling the aisle, deep-kissing the guy in front of me. Her right heel is wedged against my instep. Her right palm rests on my left knee. She's obviously too busy eating her boyfriend's face to notice. I get up, partly to go to the loo, partly to make a point. The girl extracts her tongue from his throat and looks up at me, peeved. She was just getting started.

At the back of the plane, sitting alone, I find the pop star in white clothes who was with the Swiss cops in the airport. He appears to have lost some of his self-assurance. He sits, twiddling his thumbs, looking pretty fed up. I wait outside the loo, wondering. If he's so famous that he needed protection, where's his minder? And how come none of the youngsters onboard are pestering him for an autograph? Ah, maybe he's not a pop star. Maybe he just got deported.

I turn away to watch clouds through a porthole. After a moment, a well-dressed lady exits the loo and apologizes in Romanian for the delay. I enter the toilet and stare at the seat. There are dusty shoeprints on each side. Someone has been squatting on it, in case of germs.

When we land in Bucharest everyone claps the pilot, despite the rough landing. Still, it's a nice gesture and very polite of them. In the shuttle bus, everyone seems happy to be back.

Outside the airport, taxi drivers are asking 300 lei – 100 euros – for a twenty-minute ride into town. I'm stunned. Even with my maths, it's about fifteen times over the going rate.

"No, thanks," I reply, scanning the car park. None of the decent taxis are here.

"What's your problem?" asks one of the drivers, all smiles with a gold tooth.

"300?" I reply, hauling my rucksack, "Are you kidding? I can fly to London for less."

The driver tugs his lapels and groans at me: "Yes, *Domnul...* but the traffic!"

I keep walking, turning on my mobile phone to call for a cheaper alternative. Then I stop at a tree in the circular car park, dump my rucksack and settle down to wait. The taxi driver backs off and tries his luck with a young woman emerging from the arrivals hall. But she too waves him away and drags her suitcase on wobbly little wheels towards the trees where I am waiting.

"So, they tried to rip you off as well, huh?" she asks, setting up camp nearby. She presses buttons on her mobile, looking peeved.

"Yeah," I reply.

"Never mind," she sighs, "Not all our taxi drivers are like them."

"I know. I just called one," I reply.

We exchange details of our travels, favourite cities and good places to shop. She's Romanian, just back from London. She knows all about Heathrow and we agree it is the worst airport we've ever been to. As we chat, other passengers edge past.

"Excuse me," says one, carrying heavy bags.

"Pardon me," says another, close behind.

The woman waiting near me lights a cigarette and watches them with a sceptical smile.

"What's funny?" I ask.

"Those guys were on my flight," she explains, "they're all being polite because they've been living in England for a bit. Next week they'll be back to normal, saying: *Hey you, move it!*"

"Maybe they were polite before they left?" I reply. She blows smoke, trying not to laugh.

Our taxis arrive a few minutes later and soon I'm zooming through busy traffic, where sirens wail and drivers beep and yell behind dusty windscreens. They look possessed. I chuckle to myself, wondering. Maybe she was right. My young driver watches me in the rear-view mirror.

"Bucharest! You like it?" he asks, grinning like a tour guide on commission. We pass a big old church and he crosses himself three times. For a moment, I'm tempted to do the same.

"Yeah, I think so," I reply.

Because I've had enough travelling for one summer. I've been to new places and learned some new things. Travel broadens the mind but it's always good to be home, if that's where I am. I lean forward and ask him to slow down, then I sit back to enjoy the ride.

Three Beers

"How was Iraq?" I ask.

At first, Vasile seems unsure how to respond. He opens a can of *Ursus* and carefully pours the golden beer into a tilted glass, watching the foam rise. When he's finished, he takes the can in his big hands and squashes it in a few deft moves, knuckles locked like a vice. When he's done, the beer can looks more like a beer mat. He lays it on the table. Then he answers.

"The first time was great. The Shi'ites were glad to see us. Farther north, where the Sunnis are, it was different. Saddam was their man, so you can imagine..."

He doesn't finish the sentence. Instead he lowers his close-cropped head and sips froth from the glass. He smacks his lips as tiny bubbles creep along the top of his black moustache, like a convoy of white ants. His tanned biceps are big as rugby balls. His T-shirt clings to his chest. A thick vein runs up one side of his neck. He looks as if he could walk through a brick wall without too much trouble. A car backfires in the street beyond the garden. I glance towards the sudden noise, but Vasile doesn't bat an eyelid.

"So, were you part of the invasion?" I ask.

"No, we Romanians went in a little later," he replies. "Our job was not combat, it was humanitarian. Or so we thought. It took us a while to find out what was really going on."

I'm intrigued, but also aware that too many questions might put him off. It's a fine line. So I wait and we sit in silence, enjoying a summer sunset on the terrace of his spacious home, under a canopy of dark vines. Succulent blue grapes hang down in tight bunches, full of promise.

"How do you mean?" I murmur eventually. Vasile grins. He knows what I'm up to.

"In my personal opinion," he sighs, "our mission was not really about helping Iraqis, their needs were clearly beyond our technical capabilities. No, I think our job was to help the Americans. To provide cover, a humanitarian smokescreen for the military, so they could gather intelligence. The funny thing is they were providing cover for us too. We helped each other."

"Were you a spy?" I ask. The words pop out faster than they should. Vasile is about to reply but gets distracted, looking over my shoulder towards the kitchen beyond. His two young daughters trot towards us in matching tracksuits, blue and yellow and red, with the word *Romania* embroidered on the front pockets. They look like tiny gymnasts ready for the Olympics.

"Can we watch a DVD?" asks the eldest, her head angled to one side, so he can't refuse. Vasile nods but taps his big G-Shock watch, holding up his wrist to show them. The girls trot off.

"Not spies," he continues, "more like a Trojan Horse. We'd go out, do our stuff, and the American guys would provide security. At least, that was the theory. In practice, they were tapping the local Iraqis, watching them, trying to find out where and when to expect trouble."

He twists in his chair and looks out from the terrace, checking the hilly horizon. The sunny day has darkened to dusk, the wind is picking up. Grey clouds mushroom across the sky like special effects. The heavens flash and boom far away, and then the rain starts, *pitter-pat.*

His pretty wife Monica collects our empty dinner plates. She wears a short summer dress of black and white hoops. Her tummy has a large bulge, as if she's hiding a watermelon. They're hoping for a boy this time. Her blonde hair is tied back in a band of apricot silk. She moves around the table, clearing up after the meal. My heart says I should help her, but my head says I might not get another chance for this chat. She points at Vasile's squashed beer can.

"How many is that?" she asks. Vasile holds up a stubby first finger, by way of reply.

"Good boy," she replies and walks away, carrying the plates.

"How was it the second time?" I ask.

"Awful!" replies Vasile, looking fed up. "So much had changed by then."

"Why?"

"The Iraqis hated us. You could see it in their eyes, hear it in their voices."

"Because they'd realized you couldn't help? Or because their country was falling apart?"

"Both," he says, reaching for his glass.

Monica returns carrying plates of vanilla ice-cream dripping with hot chocolate sauce. You can't beat Romanian hospitality. She sits alongside us. On my plate, I spot a brown sausage.

"*Salam de biscuiţi,*" says Monica, "made from crushed biscuits, cocoa, Turkish delight."

"And magic," adds Vasile, taking his spoon. "Try some!"

We eat in silence. Good food deserves respect. When we are done, Vasile gathers the plates and walks into the kitchen. When he returns he's carrying a fresh can of beer and a clean glass. I watch, intrigued, as he goes through the same routine with military precision. He pulls the ring and pours the amber liquid, producing a neat froth like a veteran barman. He drains the can of every drop then slowly crushes it between his hands, stopping now and then to reposition it. He doesn't speak. The process requires concentration. In moments the can is converted into a disc of crumpled aluminium. Then he places it on the dining table, alongside the first one.

"You OK, Vasi?" asks Monica. He nods and holds up two fingers. It's some kind of game.

"So, will you go back?" I ask. Vasile shrugs.

"If they send me!"

He stares at the squashed cans with dark brown eyes that don't blink.

"I heard you were in Africa too?" I ask, changing the subject. He nods.

"I was never xenophobic before that," he says, "but I was when I left."

"How come?"

"Because they were xenophobic towards us," Vasile mutters. "You ever been there?"

"Yes," I reply. I tell him briefly about my time in different African countries. Vasile raises his hands behind his head. He seems to be watching or waiting. I think I know why.

"And did you ever feel xenophobic?" he asks. Just as I expected.

"No, except…"

"Except?" he says, with a quick smile. The boot is on the other foot, now.

"The country doesn't matter," I reply, "but by the time I left, I knew I'd stayed too long. Something was changing inside me, and I didn't like it."

"How long?"

"Two and a half years, with about three week's vacation."

"Three weeks R&R?" Vasile's bushy eyebrows arc into furry bridges. "That's not enough."

"That's life with an NGO," I reply. "Burns you out – but I guess you'd know about that?"

He doesn't answer. He watches his wife as she rises from her seat, moving towards the kitchen.

"I'll get some coffee," says Monica. "Don't go telling any military secrets, Vasi."

"As if," he replies.

His two daughters bounce onto the terrace wearing bright pyjamas imprinted with Barbie Doll designs: *Beach Barbie, Gym Barbie, Office Barbie.* Each little girl is clutching a furry kitten, one black, one spotty. The little cats stare out at the world, green eyes glassy with confusion.

"Story?" asks the youngest daughter, head angled to one side, just like big sister. It's a cute tactic. Who could refuse? Not Vasile. He walks towards the girls, shepherding them back inside.

In the kitchen, I find Monica washing the dishes. I grab a dishtowel and we chat over a sink of bubbles. We talk about her job as a pharmacist, about politics and pregnancy. She's fun.

"Do you get cravings?" I ask, "I heard some women even like to eat coal."

Monica pauses for a moment and gives me a strange look.

"Urban myth," she replies. "For me, it's not about what I *like*. It's what I do *not* like."

"For example?" I ask, drying the last plate.

"Spicy food, perfume and alcohol," says Monica.

Vasile enters the kitchen and opens the fridge.

"Good idea," he says, extracting another can of *Ursus*. Then he strides away, back onto the terrace. I can easily imagine him marching on a military parade ground: chin in the air, eyes right, boots gleaming. Monica looks at me.

"How many is that?" she asks, wiping her hands. I hold three fingers in the air.

"As if," she replies, rinsing the sink with fresh water. The soap-bubbles spiral and vanish. I follow Vasile onto the terrace, where rain hammers on the corrugated metal roof above our heads like an army marching to war. We look out at a crimson sky, where battles rage.

"So Mike, how do you like being in Transylvania?" he asks, pulling at his third can.

"I love it."

"Why?"

"The people, the landscape, the history, the food…"

"You know why Mihai Viteazul united us?" says Vasile. He carefully pours his beer, raising the glass to eye-level, watching like a connoisseur, checking the angle.

"No idea."

"For money!" he replies.

"Most things happen because of money," I add. "Like Iraq, probably?"

Vasile gives me a quick look that seems to say *don't get me started.* But I can't stop.

"You've been there. You've seen what's going on. What would you tell President Bush, if you had five minutes of his time?"

Vasile laughs short and hard, like it's a good joke.

"Who, me? With Bush? I'd tell him nothing, we're not on the same planet!"

"What about the big boss, that General Petraeus? What would you say? Or ask?"

Vasile puts his glass down and takes the empty can between his hands.

"Nothing," he sighs. "In his shoes, I'd probably do the same. It's tough at the top. Anyway, you sound like a journalist. It's the week-end."

Then he slowly mashes the aluminium tube to a flat disc and places it on the table with the other two. He sits back and looks at them. He seems to be drifting to a world of his own.

"One last question," I say.

He glances up at me – *it better be*. He looks tired.

"Shoot."

"Why do you squash the beer cans?" I ask.

"He always does that," says Monica, reappearing from the kitchen, "ever since he came back from Iraq." She's carrying a tray of three tiny cups – smells like coffee. Vasile shrugs and reaches for the crumpled aluminium discs. He shuffles them like casino chips in his big hands.

"It's just a habit," he says. "We used to drink with the Belgians. Their officer would come and check how many beers everyone had. The rule was three per night. You had to put your cans in a bin and he'd look in and count them. If he found too many, there was trouble. But he wasn't very good at his job. Some of us Romanians discovered that if we squashed our cans and put them at the bottom of the bin, he wouldn't see. So, of course, the Belgian soldiers copied us. And every night their officer would come into the bar and ask *how many is that?* And the Belgians would hold up a finger or two, even though they'd had lots more. And the officer would glance in the bin. Then he'd look at us and say *how come all you Romanians drink so slowly?*"

Vasile chuckles to himself. Monica gives him a glazed look, full of love but vaguely troubled. Her husband stretches a muscular arm towards a waste-paper basket and drops the metal discs into it. They clatter like coins from a machine. He settles back in his chair and says:

"Anyway, let's talk about something else."

Romania Has Cancer

The notary in the silky polka-dot blouse charges me 200 euros for a ten-minute meeting. She prints off three documents and seals them with blobs of hot red wax, like she's Elizabeth I declaring war. Then she tells me:

"By the way, you need another stamp."

"Oh, really?" I reply, with just a hint of irony. That makes four stamps today, from different official offices around town. Not to mention queues. She seems to be reading my mind.

"This is Romania, after all," she sighs, capping her Mont Blanc pen. I'm starting to feel like a three-legged dog that everyone pities but-not-really. I back out, wagging my tail.

On the way, I notice she has a huge laminated photo of the Dynamo Bucharest team pinned to the wall behind her door. It measures four feet long by two feet high. It's pretty impressive, all those fit footy players with folded arms and big smiles, hoping for a transfer to Chelsea. I gawk at it for a moment. She must be keen. I turn and smile.

"Nice photo," I tell her. "By the way, I'm a Liverpool fan."

She gives me a look that says *I'm-married-and-you-can-go-now.*

My taxi to Piaţa Unirii takes longer than usual because all the cars slow down to get a good look at the ornamental fountains. Instead of normal water, today the fountains are gushing water coloured blue, yellow, green, pink, turquoise and red. The red one gushes in huge bloody arcs, like Dracula is spinning the brass taps of slaughter below ground. The yellow fountains look like showers of piss reaching for the sky. Presumably it's a cultural gesture. It's obviously not a complete waste of public money, because drivers are climbing out to take photos on their mobile phones and the traffic is jammed for about a kilometre each way, which is even more than usual.

I'm sitting there, roasting in the midsummer mayhem, trying to remember the word for 'pedestrian crossing' in Romanian. But I can't, so I point at the faded white stripes across the road ahead of us and ask my driver, in Romanian: "How do you say *zebra*?"

He gives me the eye – *Jesus, why me.* He looks like he needs a bed, poor guy. He's probably been razzing around Bucharest since dawn. His heavy jowls are dotted with grey stubble, his breath reeks of fags.

"*Zebra*," he replies, matter-of-factly. But something tells me he missed the point.

"No, I mean gender," I ask. "In Romanian, animals are masculine or feminine, yes?"

"How should I know?" he replies, with a shrug. "It depends if it's a boy or a girl."

The clerk in the next office scrutinizes my documents through gold-framed spectacles. I show her the three red wax seals on my expensive parchment from the notary.

"They're official. They cost me two hundred euros," I explain.

She glances up from her desk and gives me a grin. Her plastic name-tag says *Lucia.* She has brown hair cut in a neat French bob and wears a grey polo-neck sweater. Her head looks like a coconut in a fairground. She's chubby and jovial, like a favourite aunt who never forgets your birthday and says *you're as bright as a button.* But suddenly she looks puzzled and says:

"What are you, stupid? Two hundred euros? You don't need candle wax."

She reaches into a steel drawer and pulls out a yellow form, nudging it across the desk.

"You just need this."

Then she explains: first, I must fill it in. Then I must photocopy it three times. Then I must take it across town for another stamp. Then I must bring it back.

"Wow, so easy?" I ask. She gives me another grin and replies:

"By the way, the notary ripped you off. There's no charge for what you need."

Back on the street, I'm still wondering about that 200 euros. Maybe my notary is planning to buy a football team. I raise my hand and a yellow taxi squeals to a stop. The door swings open.

The middle-aged driver has a comb-over and is chewing gum as if he hasn't eaten in days. I climb aboard and try to strap myself in with the belt. But there's no clasp.

"Because you won't need a seat-belt," he says, laughing.

But in my opinion, he's wrong. Because we are soon hurtling down Calea Victoriei as though one of us is in labour. I'm so scared I can scarcely speak. It's like riding with Lewis Hamilton.

He comments on almost every car we pass: *That VW is a good deal. The Renault is not bad either.* I'm hoping he'll slow down if we chat about cars, so I try.

"I hear the Dacia Logan costs only 6,000 euros – it's the top-selling small car in Europe."

But my knowledgeable driver wrinkles his nose.

"It's a piece of shit," he replies. "No acceleration and no brakes."

I'm rather surprised by his lack of patriotism, especially as we're sitting in a Dacia Logan and we've been screaming away from traffic lights at 0-60 in 9 seconds, not to mention braking to a dead stop within 10 meters. Then I remember the Dacia is not really a Romanian vehicle, it's French, made under license from Renault. He jams the brakes yet again and we skid to a halt behind a queue of growling trucks and bikes and cars. Fifty meters ahead, the traffic lights glow like succulent strawberries. He wags a finger at me, like it's my fault we had to stop.

"Six grand? No way. You can't get a decent Dacia for less than ten," he hisses. "And for that money, you want to buy a second-hand Skoda. Like this one, see? That's what you want."

He jabs a finger ahead. The car in front is a Skoda, but I've got a better idea.

"Actually, I want to get out," I explain, thrusting money into his hand. Then I'm on the pavement. My car expert roars away down the street. The tarmac stinks of scorched rubber.

By the time I leave the next office, I'm feeling like a prisoner on his first day out of jail. I peer at the documents in my hands: *stamp, stamp: authorized, approved.* Now I can go back to *Doamna* Lucia. I can imagine her grinning as I offer my papers. I start walking, looking for a taxi.

Traffic rushes past me. On this side of the street, there is no pavement for 500 meters. It was removed for Bucharest's recent Formula 3 races, the ones that nobody attended because it rained all weekend and the seats were too costly. So the organizers let people in for free. It was the only way to get a few people in the grandstands for the TV cameras. It was a bit of a fiasco, still the races will be back every year for the next ten, it seems. But apparently, our pavement won't. The pungent stench of death seeps up my nostrils. I pinch my nose as I pass a large white street-dog, face mashed in, slumped rigid against the wall, its snout in a sticky pool of dusty black blood. It makes me wonder, because these mutts are usually pretty savvy when it comes to traffic. Probably got hit by a speeding driver, inspired by Formula 3.

My next taxi driver looks like a real hard-ass. His head is shaved to the bone. He's about 35 years old. He has a perfect tan and cold blue eyes that shimmer like subterranean pools. He's quiet, something scary about him, like he might rip you apart with his bare hands. But I'm in a hurry and climb aboard hoping I won't end up in a meat pie.

His driving is careful and precise. He checks his mirrors, indicates when overtaking and keeps a safe distance from the car in front. He doesn't say much. I tell him it's a hot day. He glances at me, knowingly – *I guess that explains why my arse is stuck to the seat.* After a bit he asks me a question. The one I never know how to answer.

"What do you think of Romania?" he mutters sideways, Bogart-style.

"Good question. What do you think of it?" I reply, trying not to sound like a smarty-pants.

"You first," he insists, with a sneaky little smile. I have a feeling he's OK after all. So I tell him what I love about Romania, and what I don't. When I'm done, he says:

"Journalist?"

"Ex," I reply.

"Thought so," he says, tapping his temple like he knows a thing or two. "And if you want my opinion", he adds, "Romania has cancer."

The phrase hangs heavy between us. I can hardly believe my ears.

"Excuse me?" I ask.

He waves a finger back and forth like a windscreen wiper at the world beyond his yellow cab.

"Look out there," he urges me. "Do you really think any of this is real? Romania is not a country. It's a stage, it's all pretend, fake!"

No wonder his eyes shimmer. I'm riding with Metaphysical Motors.

"Looks real to me," I reply. "But I suppose it depends what you mean?"

Then he's off, transformed from Silent Bob into an articulate spokesman for the downtrodden, the oppressed and the huddled masses. Including his wife, who's a lawyer.

"You wouldn't believe what she sees, the shady deals, the dodging. Makes her sick – the politicians in this country? It's a sham, a national disgrace."

"Why doesn't she resign?" I ask.

"And do what?" he snaps, easing into a sharp corner. Even though he seems unhappy, he stays cool, drives slowly.

"I don't know. Maybe she could get a new job. Or have kids – unless you've got some?"

My driver gives me a funny look, like I said the wrong thing.

"Have you ever met any kids in Bucharest?" he asks, calmly.

"One or two from my block," I reply. "They seem OK. At least, I think so."

"You think so? Listen to me – kids here don't respect anyone or anything. Not any more. When I was young, even if somebody was one year older, I always respected them. But with these kids, it's *screw you.* All they want is more computers, clothes, Coke. Do you have kids?"

"Two, but I sold them on eBay," I reply. My driver nods at me – *good idea.* But he doesn't laugh at my joke. Instead, he groans.

"This country drives me nuts. God knows why you foreigners stay. You must be mad."

I tell him he's almost right. I almost went mad today. I tell him about the queues, the stamps, forms, 200 euros down the pan. I tell him I feel like I need a psychiatrist's sofa. I'm fried.

"You don't need a psychiatrist, you just need this," he says, tapping his temple again. I'm half-expecting him to pull a yellow form out of his ear and tell me to photocopy it three times. Instead, he tells me he has two jobs: one as a taxi-driver, the other as a security guard for a German executive, VIP. And that's how he learned about psychology. From watching, listening.

"Trust me, I know that stuff. People think security is all sunglasses and breaking arms," he confides. "But if you're smart, you don't need force. You anticipate and avoid trouble."

I tell him it's impossible to avoid bureaucracy, even if you can anticipate it.

"I know bureaucracy," he answers, with a grin. "My wife is a lawyer, remember."

I am tempted to ask him whether that means she's part of the problem or part of the solution. But I don't, because we're getting on rather well and I'd rather not be in a choke-hold at the next set of traffic lights. Bucharest glides by. I feel safe in his company, I think.

"You're a good driver," I say. "Not like some taxis."

I'm hoping my compliment might cheer him up. But it doesn't.

"That's exactly what I'm talking about!" he scowls. "They have no idea how dangerous they are, for their clients. They wouldn't last five minutes in a real driving job, in your country."

"They'd get arrested by the cops," I reply. "But you shouldn't be so pessimistic. I think Europe will rub off on Romania. Democracy doesn't happen overnight. Even in Britain, it's still not right."

"Democracy in Romania?" he replies, laughing. "Maybe in 200 years! If I could leave tomorrow, I would. I'd get as far away from this place as possible."

I tell him I know decent Romanians who work abroad, make money and plan to return.

"You should try it. Maybe your influence will help?" I add. But my driver shakes his bullet-head.

"Once they go, they never come back. Not if they've got any sense."

Then he reminds me that I am overlooking something very important.

"Don't forget we're Latin, but not French or Italian. We're also Slav, but not Serbian or Russian. We're a mixture, screwed-up and insecure. We still don't know who we are, not yet. So we copy from everyone else, usually the bad bits, because that's easy. That's the problem."

Then he makes a gesture with his hand, like a snake slithering down his thigh.

"We do this, side-to-side. We can't walk straight, without..."

Then he flicks a hand at his hip, like a cowboy with a gun. But no, he means something else. Finally I get it.

"Guide wheels?" I suggest. "Like on a kid's bike?"

"*Guide wheels*, yes!" he says, dead impressed. "That's a new word for me."

Then he freezes: he's watching a long black limousine that purrs past us and jabs his finger at it.

"Who the hell has money for a Bentley in Romania? Some fat crook, I bet."

He drops me at my destination. I give him a decent tip and I climb out.

"Thanks, it was an interesting chat. But try to be positive!"

"Why?" he replies, calmly.

Walking away, I pass a familiar restaurant and I notice something odd. A few years ago, this place was a cosy café with wobbly tables and good pizzas. But everything looks different now. The cosy café has been upgraded, transformed into a swish restaurant. Somebody has obviously invested in it, spotted the business potential. Smart move – could be a prime location – city centre, lots of passing trade.

But the little wobbly tables are long gone. The door is no longer made of dull steel. It's made of dark-stained wood, with too many scratches and bumps. The window frames seem old-fashioned, Victorian. The décor is nautical – the front of the restaurant resembles the back of a Spanish galleon. Bronze lamps hang from rusty-looking chains in the lobby, casting a yellow glow. It wasn't like this in 1994. I wonder what it's called now. A faded plaque hangs above the entrance: *The Boatyard: Since 1886*. Since when?

Further up the road, the door of *Doamna* Lucia's office is now padlocked, even though the sign says *09.00-17.00.* Puzzled, I check my watch: 4.45 pm. I press my face to the thick grey glass, making desperate faces at a skinny old guy on the other side. He's in the lobby, turning off the fluorescent strip lights one by one, and with them my hope. A cigarette dangles from his free hand. I tap fingernails hard on the glass. I sound like a bird pecking at its reflection.

"*Domnul*, please! I need to see *Doamna* Lucia, she told me…"

As he flips the last switch, he turns towards me. I watch the cigarette rise to his mouth. The red tip glows brighter as he takes a long drag. He's watching me too, but not for long. He turns away and retreats into the shadows of the big old building. It's time to go home.

Cooperation

It wasn't always here, this generator. It only arrived a few weeks ago, around the back of the apartment block. It makes a racket. Chugging and chugging all day, until late. It's a big steel box about the size of a small truck but three times as loud. It's so loud that whenever I walk past it, I have to cover my ears. I look up, wondering: how on earth do the elderly residents feel – the ones who live in the apartments directly above this thing? Who does it belong to? Why is it here?

I get my answer from our Administrator, Mr. Vlaicu. He's in the lobby when I enter my block, wearing a suit and fixing yet another lurid announcement to the notice board. As usual, the sheet of paper is covered in multi-coloured felt-pen, key words underlined three times. It's a mess. Something about our central heating system – he's going to turn it on again soon, which means more bills for everyone and more paperwork for him.

"Administrator Vlaicu, why is there a generator out back?" I inquire.

"Oh, that thing," he groans, with a pin between his teeth. "It belongs to the guy who owns the shop."

"What shop?"

"The one on the ground floor, facing the street, sells printing supplies."

I know the one he means – high prices and no customers, always looks rather dubious to me.

"Why does he need a generator?" I ask. "Can't he use the power supply like the rest of us?"

The Administrator shrugs. "Last month we tried to raise his rent, first time in years. He refused, he wouldn't even negotiate. So we cut off his electricity. So he got the generator. So we're taking him to court."

"And how long will that take?" I ask. Vlaicu fixes me with his baby blue eyes.

"Years," he replies, exhaling loudly. He has nothing more to say on the matter. Then he stands back, hands on hips, admiring his notice. It looks like someone spilled a pot of paint on it.

"Doesn't anyone complain?" I ask. Vlaicu gives me an irritated look and shakes his head.

"Plenty of people, but personally I can't hear the thing upstairs. I have double-glazing. Goodbye!"

Then he is gone, vanishing into the elevator, back up to his files and folders. I look closer at the notice he pinned up, reading carefully:

On the orders of the President of the Block,

Administrator Vlaicu will lead a commission to visit all the apartments and assess the functional performance of the central heating system. Thank you for your cooperation.

The last bit is underlined in red, with a date and a time. Below the new notice, I spot an older one that looks a bit dog-eared now. I remember when Vlaicu put that one up too, a few months ago.

Silence please!

Between 2-4 pm, and 10 pm-8 am

Thank you for your cooperation.

Presumably so the old folks can have a nap, and an early night. It's underlined in red. Too bad if they live above the printer's nuclear generator and cannot afford double-glazing.

That night, in the wee small hours, I wake to a familiar drilling noise, somewhere above my head. It lasts for over a minute. I know what it is – Administrator Vlaicu urinating directly into his toilet. His bathroom is above mine. He sounds like a fruit machine spewing coins. *Chugger chugger.* What a bugger. I've already told him once. Next morning I slip a note into his mailbox:

Dear Administrator Vlaicu,

I know you aim to please, but please aim for the porcelain.

Thank you for your cooperation.

Underlined in red, maybe I'll see him in court one day.

Sunday Best

Every time I visit this place, I feel the same. Maybe it's because of the elegant flower beds, the winding paths and the chatter of happy kids. Or maybe it's the young lovers who paddle rowing boats, the skeletal old ladies who gossip on benches of battered wood or the grim-faced men who huddle around stone tables playing chess. Whatever it is, every time I walk through Cişmigiu Gardens in the centre of busy, booming Bucharest, I feel as if I'm wandering through a painting by a French Impressionist. And there is a connection, after all. Wasn't this city once known as Paris of the East? Crossing a bridge over the lake, I pause to wonder what Monet would have made of it, with his canvas and paint, some Sunday afternoon. The park was built in 1847. The first group exhibition of the Impressionists was 1874. There's a tenuous symmetry.

On the bandstand, portly men in brown military uniforms sit in concentric circles playing a medley of popular tunes for the watching crowds. The brass instruments glitter and shine in the sun. The big fat tuba curls into the air like a gilded tree. The drummer wipes sweat from the back of his neck, scarcely missing a beat. Kids dawdle about in their Sunday best, nibbling pink clouds of candy floss.

Snatches of chat float on the breeze, from middle-aged women who sit in a row, side by side, discussing last night's TV. Specifically the ins-and-outs of older men who marry young girls.

"How can she be pregnant?" asks one, sucking a sweet. "He's over sixty."

"Are you kidding?" retorts her neighbour. "Men are fertile a lot longer than us."

"It won't last," suggests another, picking knots of fluff from her worn-out black cardigan.

Further along sits a furry orange Chow dog, blue tongue hanging from its stubby snout. The dog looks like it should be guarding a Buddhist temple. Instead it's guarding the blue toilets, the ones where you have to pay. Maybe it's waiting for its master, inside on a business trip.

Turbo-folk music booms from a café terrace, where waiters in white shirts and black waistcoats glide on shiny shoes among the crowded tables, dispensing drinks and fixed smiles. Most clients are smoking. Their happy chatter and innocuous silver wisps drift across the lake. It looks like a modern-day version of Renoir's *Luncheon of the Boating Party*.

Under a large tree near the *zona de conifere,* a couple of lovers kiss passionately. The young woman sits on the man's knee. She's in her mid-twenties, slim-hipped in a short T-shirt that exposes her waist and a red thong at the rear. He's in his forties, overweight with messy hair and scuffed brown shoes, exposing his indifference to the stares of passers-by.

At the edge of the boating lake, knots of people wait quietly on the *debarcader* – the jetty – for their turn. Two tiny children are dressed in identical outfits – denim dungerees and jelly shoes. They gaze towards the centre of the lake, where a fountain spurts great arcs of water into the air, teasing them to hurry up and join the fun. One of the kids spins around, hugging herself.

The gravel crunches underfoot. The wind whispers through the leaves of a gigantic tree, easily a hundred years old. Teenagers on skates whiz down leafy avenues of smooth tarmac. Women in black crouch at the side, selling snacks and watching the energetic kids zoom by.

I find an empty bench. Before I sit down, I glance up to check the trees for pigeons, in case of sloppy bombs that will spatter on my head. Shit happens, as the Americans say. But not here and not now, I hope. I take my seat and sit back to ponder the passage of time.

This park has a place in history. It seems the name *cişmigiu* is Turkish in origin. It means the *person responsible for building or maintaining a public fountain.* And never mind the French Impressionists, Maxy, a Romanian avant-garde artist from the '20s painted *Şomeri pe o bancă în Cişmigiu: Unemployed dozing on a bench in Cişmigiu.* It's an intriguing picture with perilous perspective, a captivating blend of light and shade, action and inactivity, gossip and snoozing. It's in the National Gallery at Cluj-Napoca.

And then there's Caragiale, the Romanian writer who used Cişmigiu as the setting for stories featuring 'Mitică', the archetypal Bucharest scallywag, sly and a bit dim, but with a talent for surrealist one-liners. When a clerk loses his job, Mitică says he's been promoted to chasing flies out of Cişmigiu. Him and Beckett would get along, I reckon.

On my way out, I walk towards heavy iron gates. A stocky guy in a ragged black blazer offers to sell me a cheap watch, cracks a joke about how accurate it is. I stop to buy a tiny handful of sunflower seeds from an old lady on a wooden stool. They're still in their shells. I don't know how to eat them the way some Romanians do. I always make a mess.

As I pass through the gates to rejoin the real world of busy streets and honking traffic, I realize two things. First, Cişmigiu is not really a Monet. It's too neat, too precise for him. No, this park is more like Seurat's island of *La Grande Jatte.*

Second, I realize that like that painting, Cişmigiu too is an island, at least to me. Because it's one of the best things about Bucharest, and we're lucky Ceauşescu didn't destroy it. It's a safe haven, a quiet place for reflection, somewhere to paddle a boat, walk with friends, talk over a plan, solve a disagreement, snog someone you shouldn't.

I could come here every Sunday. In fact, maybe I will, it's not so far. Maybe I could get a job chasing flies.

4457164R00175

Printed in Great Britain
by Amazon.co.uk, Ltd.,
Marston Gate.